WELCOME

The modern carrier era, loosely defined as the period immediately before and after the collapse of the Soviet Union and end of the Cold War, has not delivered the so-called 'peace dividend' claimed and quickly cashed in by politicians keen to cut military spending in favour of more popular, vote-winning projects.

Rather, the world post-Cold War is less stable, its 'bad guys' unpredictable and unconventional in their methods of warfare. Today, an aircraft carrier is far more likely to launch strikes against terrorist insurgents than state players. After a US-led Coalition ousted invading Iraqi forces from Kuwait in 1991, for example, the US and its allies became embroiled in a long-running campaign in Iraq that evolved into an ongoing counter-insurgency against terror organisations in Iraq and Syria.

Meanwhile, the world watches anxiously as war rages between Russia and Ukraine and, not so far away, conflict between Israel and Hamas threatens to spill across the region. Over the Red Sea and Gulf of Aden, US carrier aircraft are engaged in Operation Prosperity Guardian, attempting to keep commercial shipping safe from attack off Yemen, where the Houthis are mounting a campaign nominally aimed at preventing materiel reaching Israel.

The period has also seen the US Navy complete its Nimitz Class, while introducing the new Gerald R Ford Class; China, the UK, Italy and other nations have also commissioned new aviation ships. Several familiar and respected naval aircraft types have disappeared over the past three decades, among them Grumman's A-6 Intruder, EA-6B Prowler and F-14 Tomcat, Vought's A-7 Corsair II and the BAe Sea Harrier. On the credit side, the Boeing F/A-18 Super Hornet dominates US carrier decks alongside the Lockheed Martin F-35C Lightning II, while the F-35B is the only choice for air arms looking to replace Harriers.

The new generation of naval aircraft and carriers integrates better with the fleet than ever before, the aircraft truly becoming an extension of the ship's combat reach and situational awareness. The next logical step in that development, uncrewed aircraft acting as force multipliers and combat platforms, is on the horizon, as the US Navy prepares to field Boeing's MQ-25A Stingray.

BELOW: Representing the cutting-edge present and future of US Navy aviation, USS *Gerald R Ford* launches a VFA-213 F/A-18F Super Hornet in the eastern Mediterranean Sea on October 23, 2023. US Navy

ISBN: 978 1 83632 003 6
Editor: Paul Eden
Senior editor, specials: Roger Mortimer
Email: roger.mortimer@keypublishing.com
Cover Design: Steve Donovan
Cover art and Aircraft illustrations: Andy Hay www.flyingart.co.uk
Design: SJmagic DESIGN SERVICES, India
Advertising Sales Manager: Sam Clark
Email: sam.clark@keypublishing.com
Tel: 01780 755131
Advertising Production: Becky Antoniades
Email: Rebecca.antoniades@keypublishing.com

SUBSCRIPTION/MAIL ORDER
Key Publishing Ltd, PO Box 300, Stamford, Lincs, PE9 1NA
Tel: 01780 480404
Subscriptions email: subs@keypublishing.com

Mail Order email: orders@keypublishing.com
Website: www.keypublishing.com/shop

PUBLISHING
Group CEO and Publisher: Adrian Cox

Published by
Key Publishing Ltd, PO Box 100, Stamford, Lincs, PE9 1XQ
Tel: 01780 755131 **Website:** www.keypublishing.com

PRINTING
Precision Colour Printing Ltd, Haldane, Halesfield 1, Telford, Shropshire. TF7 4QQ

DISTRIBUTION
Seymour Distribution Ltd, 2 Poultry Avenue, London, EC1A 9PU
Enquiries Line: 02074 294000.

KEY Publishing

CONTENTS

A US Marine Corps F-35B from VX-23 approaches the Royal Navy aircraft carrier HMS *Prince of Wales* over the Atlantic during the WESTLANT 23 trials series on October 11, 2023. US Navy

POWER PROJECTION

The aircraft carrier has always been a platform for power projection, a role that has gained in importance with the global instability that followed the end of the Cold War.

If the period since the UK retook the Falkland Islands from Argentine occupation is considered the modern era of carrier aviation, then the US has continued to dominate with by far the most powerful naval aviation force. The focus of naval airpower has been in the Mediterranean, Red Sea, Persian Gulf and Arabian Sea, but thanks to its large aircraft carrier fleet, the US Navy has also projected power and maintained a regular presence globally.

Since 1982, the US Navy has completed its Nimitz-class, and decommissioned the last of the Essex-, Forrestal-, Kitty Hawk and Midway-class ships, plus the unique USS *Enterprise* and USS *John F Kennedy*. Other countries have abandoned their aircraft carrier

LEFT: More than five decades since it first appeared on a carrier, the Hawkeye is more important than ever. The latest E-2D variant, represented here by a VAW-125 aircraft aboard USS *Ronald Reagan*, on station in the Philippine Sea in June 2024, is an integral, networked component in the carrier battle group's defensive shield. US Navy

programme, basing its first vessel on the partly complete Kuznetsov-class ship *Varyag*. India too purchased an ex-Soviet vessel, the modified Kiev-class ship INS *Vikramaditya* entering service in 2014. Russia continues its troublesome carrier capability with *Admiral Kuznetsov*.

Carrier aircraft

The past four decades has also seen a significant shift in operational carrier aircraft. Boeing Vertol's H-46 Sea Knight; Grumman's A-6 Intruder, EA-6B Prowler and F-14 Tomcat; McDonnell Douglas's F/A-18 Hornet; Sikorsky's H-3 Sea King; and Vought's A-7 Corsair II have all gone from US decks. France retired its Dassault Etendard and Super Etendard fleets in favour of the Dassault Rafale M, while the UK removed first the BAe Sea Harrier and then the McDonnell Douglas/ BAe Harrier II from its operations; the first-generation AV-8 Matador, a version of the original Harrier, seems to have faded from Thai service.

Interestingly, the Grumman E-2 Hawkeye remains on US and French carrier decks, looking very much as it did 40 plus years ago, even as combat airpower has shifted to a handful of types. The US Navy relies on the Boeing F/A-18 Super Hornet and EA-18G Growler and Lockheed Martin F-35C Lightning II, while **»**

capability, Argentina and Brazil among them, while Thailand's carrier no longer operates fixed-wing aircraft, and the UK left the game in 2010 and rejoined a decade later.

More recently, the UK's new fleet of Queen Elizabeth-class carriers has been commissioned, as has the first of a new class of US ship, USS *Gerald R Ford*. France switched operations from the outgoing *Clemenceau* to the new vessel *Charles de Gaulle*, while Spain now nominally operates its Harriers from *Juan Carlos I*, having scrapped *Principe de Asturias*. Italy, meanwhile, launched *Cavour* in 2004 and operates it alongside *Giuseppe Garibaldi*.

China is in the early stages of an ambitious aircraft carrier

LEFT: Helicopters fly critical enabling missions around the carrier battle group, including the all-important plane guard task, where a helicopter is in the air, ready to recover the crew of any aircraft entering the water during flying operations. The movement of mail and supplies is another important job and here an HSC-14 MH-60S transfers cargo from the Lewis and Clark-class dry cargo and ammunition ship USNS *Washington Chambers* to USS *Abraham Lincoln*, under way in the Pacific on July 23, 2024. US Navy

the US Marine Corps operates the short take-off/vertical landing (STOVL) F-35B. The F-35B also equips the UK's carriers and while the Leonardo Merlin has replaced the Royal Navy's Westland Sea Kings, variations on the Sikorsky H-60 Seahawk have taken the H-3's place in US service.

Operational focus

At least one US Navy aircraft carrier has been engaged in combat around the Gulf region, sailing the Red Sea, Persian Gulf and Arabian Sea, since 1991. Operations against Iraq that year set off a chain of events leading to the continuing fight against terrorist forces in Iraq

LEFT: The F-35 brings a step change in capability to US Navy, UK and Italian aircraft carriers. This VFA-125 F-35C was preparing to launch from USS *Nimitz* in the Pacific Ocean, during July 2024. US Navy

and Syria. Ships in the region also launched strikes into Afghanistan for years after the 9/11 terror attacks on the US and in December 2023 a new area of concern was added, off Yemen, where Operation Prosperity Guardian continues its effort to keep international shipping safe from Houthi attack.

In recent years, however, the US and UK have increasingly perceived China as an emerging threat. The country's claims on Taiwan have become bolder and Chinese ships and aircraft more aggressive in their manoeuvres, prompting the US to reinforce its military capability in the region, including regular, overt carrier deployments.

Few actions say more about international relations than exercising with a US Navy carrier

LEFT: Super Hornets, F-35Cs, Hawkeyes and Seahawks represent the modern air wing aboard USS *Abraham Lincoln*, in the Pacific Ocean on August 2, 2024. US Navy

LEFT: Exercise Nordic Response 24, part of Steadfast Defender, demonstrated European aircraft carrier interoperability, with Italy's *Giuseppe Garibaldi* (foreground) and HMS *Prince of Wales* working together. The Italian navy and UK both operate the F-35B and several variants of the Merlin helicopter, or AW101 as it is to the Italians. LPhot Belinda Alker/© UK MoD Crown Copyright 2024

LEFT: USS *George Washington* was sailing south of Japan in November 2014 when it launched this VFA-102 F/A-18F colourfully marked as the 'CAG bird'. Training operations and regular regional deployments like this help show US support, in this case for Japan, in contested waters. US Navy

battle group and the mere presence of a Nimitz-class ship is often sufficient to reassure, impress and, when necessary, intimidate. Regular global deployments therefore include frequent exercises with foreign militaries and the same is true for the navies of France, Italy and the UK, albeit on a far smaller scale.

A strong presence also sends messages of support to allies and deterrence to foes in times of conflict. Italy, France, the UK and US have all completed aircraft carrier exercises, often jointly, in Mediterranean, Aegean and Norwegian waters either as Russia was building forces on Ukraine's border or since its 2022 invasion. An increasingly belligerent Russia under President Vladimir Putin is a concern globally.

On the other hand, it should not be forgotten that an aircraft carrier has the capability to deliver multi-role capability virtually anywhere, quickly, and that has great significance to humanitarian assistance/disaster response (HA/DR) operations. The US Navy's amphibious assault ships, which might easily be reclassified as light aircraft carriers, are particularly good HA/DR platforms thanks to their role fit and fleets of Bell Boeing MV-22B Osprey tiltrotors and variety of helicopters. Reconfiguring the air wing of any carrier can quickly turn it from war machine to HA/DR hub, however, and aircraft carriers train regularly with helicopters from other services and nations to keep interoperability skills sharp.

Looking ahead, it seems likely that China will emerge as the second most powerful carrier nation after the US, but it is difficult to imagine how any incumbent could match the US Navy's decades long experience and expertise.

In the post-Cold War world, politicians looked to what they considered the relative peace and calm created by the end of East-West antagonism to reduce military spending. This affected carrier aviation as much as anything else and all navies, including the US, are still struggling to recover, in a world less stable and ever more unpredictable than it was during the uneasy status quo of the Cold War.

BELOW: Exercise Steadfast Defender 24 saw HMS *Prince of Wales* operating in Norwegian fjords during March 2024. With F-35Bs embarked, the carrier represented a major demonstration of European NATO strength – Norway shares a border with Russia. LPhot Edward Jones/© UK MoD Crown Copyright 2024

FURY, DEMOCRACY AND EL DORADO CANYON

Three smaller US operations in the 1980s and 1990s illustrated the global reach and presence of the country's aircraft carrier fleet.

Although they had played a vital role during the Vietnam War, US aircraft carriers had effectively served as floating air bases, remaining in the same patch of water for months on end. The same might be said of Operation Desert Storm in 1991, once the initial Operation Desert Shield dash into theatre had concluded, but two 1980s' actions and another, more unusual deployment in 1994, demonstrated the invaluable ability of the aircraft carrier to deliver airpower quickly and at range.

1983: Operation Urgent Fury

In October 1983, the self-styled People's Revolutionary Army (PRA) arrested and executed Grenada's prime minister, Maurice Bishop, who had taken power in the island nation after a coup in 1979. The new leadership, led by the PRA's General Hudson Austin, enjoyed extensive support from Cuba, including military advisors and a handful of Soviet special forces soldiers.

On October 23, several Caribbean nations called on the US for assistance, their plea reinforced by Governor General Sir Paul Scoon, representative of HM The Queen in Grenada. The US immediately switched its planning from an evacuation of US and other nationals to a military assault, codenamed Operation Urgent Fury. Large numbers of US Army troops and Marines were employed, along with extensive naval, army and US Air Force aviation assets, while the amphibious assault ship USS *Guam* was positioned as a base for CH-46 and CH-53 assault helicopters and their AH-1T escorts. Fixed-wing airpower came from USAF AC-130 gunships and the aircraft of Carrier Air Wing 6 in USS *Independence*.

A simultaneous amphibious, helicopter and parachute assault was delivered on October 24, inserting troops at multiple locations. US Navy air support came primarily from A-7E Corsair II and A-6 Intruder attack aircraft flying off *Independence*.

This was an era when precision attack remained in its infancy and communication between units, especially over a fast-moving battle, was frequently fragmented. As a result, one A-7 erroneously bombed a large building from which the pilot

believed his jet had taken anti-aircraft fire – it turned out to be a hospital and there were many civilian casualties. Just 48 hours later, another A-7E mistakenly strafed US troops.

Several helicopters were lost, including examples of the US Marine Corps' AH-1T and CH-46E, while 19 personnel were killed. The island was returned to democratic rule, however, and the action considered a success.

1986: Operation El Dorado Canyon

The US maintained military bases in Libya until 1967, when it withdrew in the face of rising nationalism. In 1969, Colonel Muammar Gaddafi overthrew the country's government and was soon forging links with the USSR. Vehemently opposed to Imperialism, Gaddafi funded terrorist organisations intent on attacking what he saw as his Imperialist enemies, the UK and US among them.

In October 1973, he extended Libya's territorial waters in a move unrecognised by the world; Libyan fighters fired on a USAF C-130 as a result. Refusing to accept Gaddafi's artificial boundary, the US Navy regularly exercised within it and encounters between Libyan aircraft and those flying off US carriers were frequent.

The situation briefly escalated on August 19, 1981, when two VF-41 Tomcats destroyed a pair of Sukhoi Su-22 *Fitter-J* attack aircraft in a still controversial engagement. Although the immediate

situation appeared to calm, Gaddafi continued expanding his support for terrorism, especially the Palestine Liberation Organization (PLO). In 1995, the US warned that terrorist action would elicit a military response which might be against Libya. Rather than backing down, Gaddafi declared a 'Line of Death' across the gulf of Sidra, reinforcing his 1973 action.

Determined to continue asserting its right to freedom of navigation, the US Navy tested Gaddafi's resolve with 'incursions' under a campaign dubbed Operation Prairie Fire. On March 24, 1986, Libya fired on a US aircraft and the guilty SA-5 missile battery received attention from HARM-firing A-7E Corsair IIs as a result. The Libyan navy responded with surface combatants – two »

ABOVE: Helicopters, including this US Marine Corps CH-53D, were key to Operation Urgent Fury. US Marine Corps

LEFT: The F/A-18A entered combat for the first time on April 15, 1986. VFA-132 and VMFA-323 both flew the type off USS *America*. US Navy

BELOW: Flying off USS *Independence*, VA-87 used its A-7Es over Grenada. Armed with cluster munitions and unguided bombs, this aircraft was over the island late in October 1983. US Navy

A-6E Intruders sank a patrol boat, while another similar vessel and a corvette fell victim to the Grumman type later that day and on the 25th.

On April 5, 1986, a Berlin disco was bombed. Libya was thought to be involved and since the attack killed a US serviceman, the US justified a strike on Libya as self-defence.

Codenamed Operation El Dorado Canyon, it was planned as a coordinated series of attacks by US Air Forces Europe F-111s and US Navy jets. The F-111s flew from bases in the UK, while USS *Coral Sea* and USS *America* launched the naval assets. Several intelligence gathering and command and control aircraft, including Hawkeyes, monitored the operation, protected as they did so by F-14s.

Coral Sea sent eight A-6Es against the airfield at Benina, accompanied by an EA-6B for jamming, plus six US Navy and Marine Corps F/A-18As and six A-7Es for defence suppression – this was the Hornet's combat debut. Four MiG-23 *Floggers*, two Mi-8 *Hip* helicopters and a Fokker F27 transport were destroyed. Meanwhile, six A-6Es and an EA-6B from USS *America* went to Al Jamahiriyak Barracks and bombed successfully.

Tension continued to simmer even after El Dorado Canyon, reaching its head again on January 4, 1989. This time USS *John F Kennedy* and its battle group were exercising their right to freedom of navigation when a pair of Libyan MiG-23s was judged to have belligerent intent. They were downed by two F-14s. With Iraq rising as a new concern and a lessening of PLO activity after Israel and the Palestinians agreed on a peace deal, US-Libya antagonism waned into the 1990s and no further military engagement took place until 2011.

1994: Operation Uphold Democracy

Almost the operation that never was, Uphold Democracy was mounted from September 19, 1994, to ensure the return of Haiti to democratic rule. In December 1990, Jean-Bertrand Aristide had been elected president after a period of military rule. Unhappy with his reformist policy, the military mounted a coup in 1991. Keen to return the

ABOVE: An E-2C launches off USS *Saratoga*, most likely close to Libya in March 1986. US Navy

LEFT: About to catapult from USS *America*'s deck off the Libyan coast, this F-14A is armed with AIM-9 AAMs underwing and AIM-7 under the fuselage. US Navy

LEFT: USS *Saratoga* was involved in freedom of navigation exercises, crossing the so-called Line of Death into the Gulf of Sidra in March 1986. Its Tomcats failed to find air-to-air 'trade'. US Navy

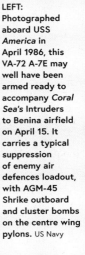
island to democracy, in 1994 the US intervened.

A significant troop presence was deemed necessary to ensure fair elections and USS *Dwight D Eisenhower* exchanged its air wing for a large contingent of US Army UH-60A and AH-1 helicopters. These were in action on September 19, when 2,000 troops went ashore.

Aristide won the presidential election, but General Raoul Cedras was initially reluctant to step down. As the US prepared to invade, President Jimmy Carter intervened and Cedras was persuaded to leave office on October 15.

LEFT: Photographed aboard USS *America* in April 1986, this VA-72 A-7E may well have been armed ready to accompany *Coral Sea's* Intruders to Benina airfield on April 15. It carries a typical suppression of enemy air defences loadout, with AGM-45 Shrike outboard and cluster bombs on the centre wing pylons. US Navy

LEFT: USS *Saratoga* tangled with Libya in March 1986, its Intruders sinking three Libyan navy vessels. Here a VA-85 A-6E recovers during in-theatre operations. US Navy

BELOW: Looking somewhat unusual with its deck covered in drab green US Army AH-1 and UH-60A helicopters, USS *Dwight D Eisenhower* manoeuvres ready to depart for Haiti and Operation Uphold Democracy. The vessel also had 1,800 soldiers of the US Army's 10th Mountain Division embarked. US Navy

GRUMMAN F-14 TOMCAT

Arguably the most distinctive and best known carrier aircraft of the modern era, the F-14 Tomcat was retired from US Navy service in 2006.

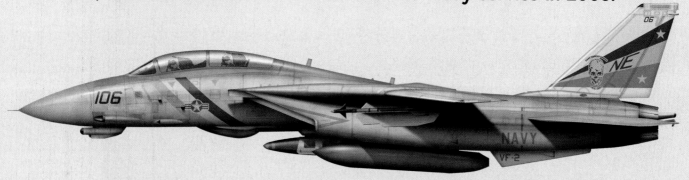

BELOW: A VF-32 'Swordsmen' F-14B launches off USS *Harry S. Truman* for an Operation Iraqi Freedom mission on December 26, 2004. The lack of in-theatre air threat meant the Tomcat was performing in the close air support and then-new intelligence, surveillance and reconnaissance (ISR) roles. US Navy

Almost two decades since its withdrawal from carrier operations, Grumman's F-14 Tomcat continues to epitomise US Navy aviation in popular culture thanks to the 1986 movie 'Top Gun'; only time will tell if the 2022 sequel 'Top Gun: Maverick' raises the Super Hornet to a similar level of fame.

Even by the standards of the long aircraft development programmes typical of the modern era, the Tomcat's was a lengthy gestation. It began in the summer of 1957, when the US Navy began its AAM-N-10 Eagle long-range

air-to-air missile (AAM) project. The Navy was not alone in its expectation that future air combat would rely on missiles, with opposing aircraft engaging over ranges so distant that their pilots might never see the enemy machine. In this context, the platform was secondary to the weapon system and the choice of the Douglas F6D Missileer in December 1960 ill fated.

Planned for a pair of Pratt & Whitney TF30 turbofans, the straight-winged F6D was optimised to carry and launch six Eagles from a loiter position someway distant from its parent carrier. The F6D's rather pedestrian design suggested a machine equipped for load carrying rather than manoeuvre and the question of how an F6D might

LEFT: The second, fourth and 12th Tomcat prototypes joined for this formation around 1972. After the first prototype was lost on its second flight, prototype number 12 was numbered '1' and took over the high-speed handling trials originally assigned to the premier aircraft. US Navy

escape an attacking fighter at close range was among those that led to its abandonment before even a prototype was built.

Nonetheless, the US Navy considered the Missileer as a component within an ambitious wider system integrating advanced weapons and radar into an airframe supported by dedicated airborne early warning aircraft and ship-based sensors. That concept is familiar in today's carrier air wings, where the E-2 Hawkeye continues as the long-range radar and control support to the Super Hornet and F-35C, working alongside the ship-based Aegis Combat System. As the 1960s dawned, the ambition proved too expensive and the »

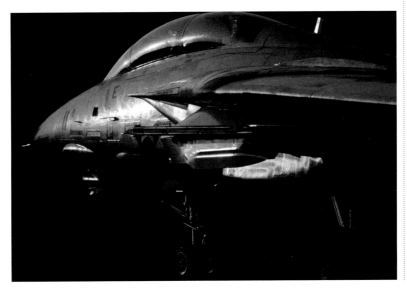

LEFT: The F-14A was built in multiple variants according to production block, with antennas and especially the sensor cluster under the nose varying through the production run. US Navy

BELOW: This VF-14 F-14A had just been waved off the deck of USS *John F. Kennedy* when this 1975 image was captured. US Navy

technological challenge too great, however, and the F6D was cancelled in December 1961.

Air Force Contribution

Meanwhile, the US Air Force had been working on its own GAR-9 missile and ASG-18 radar system for the North American F-108 Rapier. After the F-108 was cancelled in September 1959, its weapons system was adapted for the AAM-N-10 Eagle, creating the AIM-47 for the Lockheed YF-12A. Although it benefitted from the extraordinary performance of the A-12 upon which it was based, the YF-12A proved little more than an expensive project.

By now seeking a replacement for the F-4 Phantom II in the interceptor role, the Navy was inching towards what would become the F-14, with the TF30-engined General Dynamics F-111B. Designed for the combination of AN/AWG-9 and AIM-54 Phoenix refined out of the previous rounds of US Navy and Air Force development, the F-111B was doomed to fail as a carrierborne interceptor. Funded by politicians seeking to economise through a joint programme for a long-range USAF strike aircraft and a naval interceptor, the F-111B was too large and too heavy for carrier decks.

The F-111B was already struggling when the US Navy commissioned Grumman to investigate advanced fighter designs during 1966. In October 1967, Grumman offered a new airframe equipped with the AN/AWG-9 and Phoenix and powered by TF30 engines; in 1968, the F-111B was cancelled, after three years' flying and the loss of three out of seven aircraft.

VFX = F-14

Grumman's new proposal formed the basis of its bid to satisfy a new US Navy requirement, published in July 1968. Known as VFX, it specified an aircraft armed with a maximum of six Phoenix missiles or a combination of Phoenix, Sparrow and Sidewinder AAMs, plus an internal gun. Mach 2.2 performance was expected, and the aircraft needed to seat its two-man crew in tandem. Grumman's entry emerged victorious as the F-14.

Like the F-111, the F-14 had variable geometry wings. Complex from an engineering standpoint, swept back these allowed high speeds for interceptions at long range, while in the forward and intermediate positions they improved the F-14's manoeuvrability for dogfighting and slowed its approach speed for safer carrier landings. Swept fully forward, the wings also improved the jet's loiter time, meaning it could provide

TOMCAT DATA

F-14A

Length	19.10m (62ft 8in)
Wingspan, unswept	19.54m (64ft 1.5in)
Wingspan, swept	11.65m (38ft 2.5in)
Wingspan, over swept	10.15m (33ft 3.5in)
Height	4.80m (16ft)
Empty weight	18,191kg (40,104lb)
Maximum take-off weight	32,659kg (72,000lb)
Maximum weapon load	6,577kg (14,500lb)
Maximum speed	Mach 2.38
Maximum climb rate	152m/s (30,000ft/min)
Combat radius with six AIM-7 and four AIM-9	1,231km (765 miles)
Engines	Two P&W TF30-P-414A turbofans each rated at 93kN (20,900lb) with afterburner
Armament	One internal 20mm M61A1 Vulcan cannon; typical load of two AIM-54 Phoenix, two AIM-9 Sidewinder and two AIM-7 Sparrow AAMs

F-14D

As F-14A unless otherwise specified	
Empty weight	19,838kg (43,735lb)
Max take-off weight	34,473kg (76,000lb)
Combat radius with six AIM-7 and four AIM-9	1,994km (1,239 miles)
Engines	Two GE F110-GE-400 turbofans each rated at 104.98kN (23,600lb) with afterburner
Armament	One internal 20mm M61A1 Vulcan cannon; typical air-to-air load of two AIM-54, two AIM-9 and two AIM-7 AAMs; air-to-ground stores included Mk 80-series unguided bombs, Paveway-series LGBs, Mk 7-series cluster munitions and JDAM
Total production of all models	712

TOMCAT TIMELINE

First flight YF-14A – December 14, 1970	
First fleet F-14A delivered to VF-124 – October 8, 1972	
First flight F-14B – September 12, 1973	
First cruise began – September 12, 1974	
First F-14A delivered to Iran – January 27, 1976	
First flight F-14B Super Tomcat – July 14, 1981	
Two Libyan Su-22 *Fitters* shot down – August 19, 1981	
Operation El Dorado Canyon – April 15, 1986	
Top Gun movie released – May 16, 1986	
First flight F-14A+ – September 29, 1986	
First flight F-14D – April 29, 1988	
Two Libyan MiG-23 *Floggers* shot down – January 4, 1989	
Operation Desert Shield – 1990-91	
Operation Desert Storm – 1991	
Iraqi Mi-8 *Hip* shot down – February 6, 1991	
First fleet squadrons converted to F-14D – July 1992	

TOMCAT TIMELINE

Operation Southern Watch – 1992-2003

Operation Sky Monitor – 1992

Operation Deny Flight – 1993-95

Operation Northern Watch – 1997-2003

Operation Desert Fox – 1998

Operation Allied Force – 1999

Operation Enduring Freedom – 2001-06

Operation Iraqi Freedom – 2003-06

Final US Navy combat mission – February 8, 2006

US Navy retirement – September 22, 2006

Iran retains limited F-14 capability – 2024

TOMCAT VARIANTS

YF-14A – prototypes, TF30-P-412 engines, 12 produced

F-14A – primary production variant, AWG-9/AIM-54 weapon system, TF30-P-412, then -412A and later production -414 engines, 545 produced

F-14A (TARPS) – wired for TARPS, 45 built, up to 25 produced by conversion

F-14B – Seventh YF-14A modified with P&W F401-PW-400 engines

F-14B Super Tomcat – F-14B re-engined with GE F101-DFE engines

F-14A+ (F-14B from May 1, 1991) – GE F110-GE-400 engines, five F-14As and the F-14B re-engined for trials, 38 built, 48 produced by conversion from F-14A

F-14D – based on F-14+, digital avionics, enhanced air-to-ground capability, 37 built, 18 produced by conversion from F-14A

F-14D(R) – F-14A upgrade, 18 produced

NF-14D – F-14D permanently modified for trials, four produced

a persistent defensive barrier far out from the carrier battlegroup. An unusual oversweep position was also available, not for use inflight but for reducing the big aircraft's footprint on the carrier deck.

Grumman developed new manufacturing techniques for the F-14 airframe, but it was always compromised by the TF30 engine. When it issued a development contract for the F-14 Tomcat on January 14, 1969, the US Navy considered the TF30 an interim powerplant, but almost 20 years elapsed before a Tomcat served with any other engine.

Much technology had already been tested on the F-111B and the Tomcat therefore reached its first flight milestone quickly, in December 1970. Given the complexity of the technology and engineering, however, its soaring costs were unsurprising, while accidents further challenged the programme. The beginning of the end of the US Navy's quest to field an interceptor designed around a weapons system finally arrived in 1973, when VF-124 began training F-14 crews at Naval Air Station (NAS) Miramar, California.

Production ramped up slowly, although sufficient aircraft were available for VF-1 and VF-2 to take the Tomcat into combat just as the Vietnam War was ending. »

BELOW: Taken in the hangar bay aboard USS *Nimitz*, this photograph shows how the oversweep function allowed Tomcats to be packed closely together. US Navy

LEFT: The Super Hornet replaced the last US Navy Tomcats. VF-2 'Bounty Hunters' returned to NAS Oceana, Virginia on May 31, 2003, after a seven-month deployment in USS *Constellation* supporting Operations Iraqi Freedom, Enduring Freedom and Southern Watch. Back at Oceana, the unit had been transitioning into the Super Hornet equipped VFA-2 and a specially painted F/A-18F Super Hornet met VF-2's F-14D CAG bird as it flew home. US Navy

Embarked in USS *Enterprise* on September 17, 1974, the squadrons flew combat air patrols (CAP) over the Tonkin Gulf region. The F-14's operational potential was quickly apparent, but challenges in supporting the aircraft were revealed, as was its propensity for failure. Predictably, the TF30 performed poorly, with flameouts and inflight explosions not uncommon and it remained troublesome even as other aspects of the Tomcat's serviceability improved.

New engine

Aside from its high failure rate, the TF30 also lacked power in its F-14 application, meaning afterburner was required for every take-off,

with implications for fuel burn and creating further serviceability challenges. Responding to its intention of making the TF30 an interim engine, in 1973 the US Navy and Grumman flew the F-14B, the seventh F-14 prototype re-engined with the Pratt & Whitney F401-PW-400 engines. The Tomcat programme was already attracting criticism for its cost overrun, however, and the project was abandoned.

In 1981, the same aircraft was fitted with General Electric F101-DFE turbofans as the F-14B Super Tomcat. Productionised as the F110-GE-400, the new engine subsequently powered F-14+ (F-14B) and F-14D aircraft produced by conversion from F-14A

and through new production. Thanks to the F110-GE-400's increased thrust, some catapult launches were possible without afterburner and the aircraft was able to maintain energy better during fighter manoeuvres.

The 'digital' F-14D also introduced the APG-71 radar, the combination of new engine and modern radar bringing the Tomcat closer to the aircraft it had always promised to be. The AN/AWG-9 was a game-changing weapons system when it worked, but it was also challenging to maintain, especially at sea. Nonetheless, it was the cornerstone of US Navy air defence, albeit in the blue-water environment the service had expected to be its Cold War

BELOW: The F-111B proved its carrier compatibility during trials on USS *Coral Sea* but was ultimately unsuited to naval operations. US Navy

Iranian Service

Then aligned to the West, from 1976 Iran received 79 F-14A Tomcats, large numbers of Phoenix missiles and assistance with supporting infrastructure. The aircraft flew extensive combat against Iraq during the 1980-88 Iran-Iraq War, scoring tens of 'kills'.

After the Shah was overthrown in 1979, the US ceased its support for the F-14 and other systems, but Iran has continued flying its Tomcats. An increasing level of indigenous content has allowed the Islamic Republic of Iran Air Force to overcome the lack of spare parts, avionics and even weapons, and a small number of F-14s is likely to remain operational in 2024.

battleground. When it came to littoral and overland operations, Operation Desert Storm showed that the F-14 weapons system and operational doctrine left the Tomcat less well suited to combat.

The F-14D might have excelled as a modern fleet interceptor, but the US Navy was already reducing operational Tomcat numbers in favour of the multi-role F/A-18 Hornet. Instead, the F-14 community looked to extend the jet's service by dropping bombs, potentially augmenting the A-6 Intruder and compensating for the Hornet's short legs on longer-ranged missions. The effort had begun in 1988 and F-14 squadrons began hanging unguided ordnance on their aircraft during 1990.

The 'Bombcat' was too late for Desert Storm but went to sea in October 1992. Laser-guided munitions added precision attack to the Bombcat's capabilities when third party designation was available, and on September 5, 1994, VF-41 dropped GBU-16 LGBs on Serbian

targets designated by F/A-18s. Later, the LANTIRN targeting pod was integrated with the F-14D, for autonomous laser designation while also providing GPS data for navigation and laser cueing.

When the US launched Operation Enduring Freedom in 2001, the Bombcat's long range made it the preferred platform against targets

in Afghanistan, although the Coalition rapidly assembled tanker forces in the region and the US Navy switched operations to the Hornet and still-new Super Hornet. The Tomcat's inexorable progress towards withdrawal continued until September 22, 2006, when a VF-213 jet performed the F-14's final flight in US Navy service.

ABOVE: Its inflight refuelling probe extended, an F-14D manoeuvres behind a USAF tanker during an Operation Enduring Freedom mission. Typical of the configuration in which the Tomcat saw out its service, a 2,000lb Paveway II LGB is evident under the fuselage, while the right-wing station mounts a LANTIRN targeting pod. US Air Force

LEFT: The flight line at NAS Oceana, ready for the final return of the F-14 from operational deployment in March 2006. US Navy

LEFT: The seventh F-14 prototype was re-engined for a second time as the F-14B Super Tomcat. US Navy

DESERT STORM

The US Navy made a massive commitment to Operations Desert Shield and Desert Storm, stationing carriers in the Persian Gulf and Red Sea.

RIGHT: Desert Storm was among the last major conflicts in which US tactical aircraft employed unguided ordnance en masse. This VA-72 A-7E is carrying eight 500lb Mk 82 bombs equipped with retarding tail units that extended on release to slow the bombs' travel and allow the low-flying attack aircraft time to escape debris thrown up by their explosion. VA-72 flew off USS *John F Kennedy* in the Red Sea. US Navy

BELOW: VFA-81 F/A-18Cs take fuel from a USAF KC-135E Stratotanker during a Desert Storm mission. US Air Force

Founded as an autonomous sheikdom in 1756, Kuwait's origins lay in a settlement as much as 5,000 years old. The arrival of the British East India Trading Company in 1776 brought Kuwait into the British Empire and in 1899 it became a self-governed protectorate, a state of largely autonomous rule able to call upon protection from Britain.

In 1914, Kuwait's leadership was recognised as an 'independent government under British protection', while border agreements between 1922 and 1933 set its boundaries with Iraq and Nejd (Saudi Arabia from 1932). Kuwait's fortunes literally changed with the discovery of oil in 1938 and in June 1961 it gained independence, although the UK stood ready to commit military support if requested.

The request came quickly. On June 25, Iraqi leader Abdul Qarim Qassem claimed Kuwait as part of Iraq and mobilised troops. The UK responded immediately and the Iraqi advance halted. The situation remained calm until 1968, when the Arab

Socialist Ba'ath Party seized power in Iraq after a coup. The country's new vice president, Saddam Hussein worked to undermine its president, Ahmed Hassan al-Bakr, finally taking his position in 1979.

A belligerent leader, in 1980 Hussein invaded Iran, the Iraqi advance quickly degenerating into brutal stalemate and continuing until a UN-brokered July 19, 1988 ceasefire. Disengaged from Iran, Hussein quickly returned to the old enmity against Kuwait. On July 16,

1990, Tariq Aziz, Hussein's foreign minister, declared that Kuwait and the United Arab Emirates were tapping into Iraq's oil reserves and forcing reduced oil prices to harm its economy while also targeting aggression against the country.

On July 18, Iraq declared that some of Kuwait was Iraqi land and demanded reparations against 'stolen' profit for oil produced in the region. Kuwait requested Arab League political intervention the next day, while the Saudi military was placed

on alert on the 23rd. On July 25, April Glaspie, US ambassador to Iraq, met Hussein. The precise details of what was said in that meeting remain unknown, but she is believed to have asked why there was an Iraqi military build-up to the south and to have stated the US intention not to become involved. That intention clearly did not extend to standing by should Iraq invade its neighbour.

A round of economic and political wrangling between the Organisation of the Petroleum Exporting »

Countries (OPEC), Iraq and the US followed as Iraqi troops moved up to the Kuwait border, and Iraq's leadership additionally claimed the Kuwaiti islands of Bubiyan and Warba. Hussein was tipped over the edge by an August 1 meeting, in which Iraq demanded that US$5.5 billion in loans provided by Kuwait during the Iran-Iraq war should be written off. Kuwait refused and at 02:00 local time on August 2, 1990, Iraq invaded.

As Iraqi troops swept through Kuwait and up to the Saudi border, The Emir of Kuwait and his government fled to Saudia Arabia. Later that day, UN Resolution 660 called for the withdrawal of Iraqi forces. The US froze Iraqi and Kuwaiti assets and banned trade with both countries.

Recognising the immediate threat to his country, on August 6, King Fahd requested military assistance from Saudi Arabia's allies. On the 7th, Operation Desert Shield was launched when US Air Force F-15C/D Eagles departed Langley Air Force Base (AFB), Virginia, for Saudi Arabia, a coalition of forces hot on their heels.

The first US Navy aircraft carriers into theatre, USS *Independence* and USS *Dwight D Eisenhower* were toward the end of their respective cruises. They served a Desert Shield stint therefore, but did not join combat.

Passed on November 29, 1990, UN Security Council Resolution 678 authorised the use of 'all necessary means' to free Kuwait if Iraqi forces had not withdrawn by January 15, 1991. After crisis talks between Tariq Aziz and US Secretary of State James Baker on January 9 failed, the only option was war. The Coalition did

ABOVE: A VFA-81 F/A-18 hauls six unguided bombs to an Iraqi target. US Navy

LEFT: Unique to the A-7 during Desert Storm, AGM-62 Walleye was a large weapon. Here a VA-72 Corsair is about to launch from USS *John F Kennedy*. US Navy

LEFT: Apparently configured for tanking, a VA-75 A-6E works with cluster bomb-toting VA-46 Corsairs. The formation was launched by USS *John F Kennedy*, demonstrating a carrier's ability to deliver complete sets of mission assets. US Navy

not act on the January 15 deadline, but at 02:38hrs on the 17th the attack began, spearheaded by US special forces and F-117A stealth fighters.

The carriers

Six US Navy carriers engaged in Desert Storm. USS *Midway* and USS *Ranger* were stationed in the Persian Gulf, while USS *Saratoga*, USS *America*, USS *John F Kennedy* and USS *Theodore Roosevelt* sailed in the Red Sea.

Each of their carrier air wings typically included two squadrons of F-14 Tomcats, two light-attack squadrons of F/A-18 Hornets or, in its combat swan song, A-7 Corsair IIs, one or two attack squadrons of A-6E Intruders, another type at the twilight of its career, plus single squadrons of E-2 Hawkeyes, EA-6B Prowlers, S-3 Vikings and SH-3H Sea Kings. Among the Tomcats, one unit on each ship usually had two or more jets wired for the Tactical Airborne Reconnaissance Pod System (TARPS).

Desert Storm was the first conflict to see widescale use of laser-guided weapons. The A-6E TRAM (Target Recognition Attack, Multisensor) Intruder carried forward-looking infrared and laser designation systems in an undernose turret and was therefore ideally placed for precision attack. A mix of guided and unguided ordnance was expended as a result, and the US Navy exclusively debuted the AGM-84E Stand-off Land Attack Missile (SLAM) from the type. Seven of these advanced, but developmentally immature cruise missiles were launched from A-6Es. The Intruder was also proof that Iraqi anti-aircraft artillery (AAA) demanded respect, with at least one US Navy A-6E shot down and another damaged.

Each A-6 unit included the KA-6D tanker on its roster, while another A-6 evolution, the EA-6B Prowler, was better represented. Although AAA could be effective locally, the Iraqi integrated air defence system was crippled by interruption to radar systems and communication through jamming. Radar operators were also wary of switching their equipment on for fear of Coalition suppression of ⟫

ABOVE: Tomcats from VF-33, VF-84 and VF-14 take fuel from a USAF KC-10A Extender.
US Navy

BELOW: Considering its mix of air-to-air weapons, the Tomcat brought unique capability to Desert Storm. This VF-32 F-14A, up from USS *John F Kennedy*, has AIM-9 and AIM-7 underwing and at least one AIM-54 under its fuselage.
US Navy

enemy air defences (SEAD) aircraft launching anti-radiation missiles. The EA-6B was at the forefront of the effort.

Typically equipped with three or four ALQ-99 jamming pods, the Prowler often also took one or two AGM-88 High-Speed Anti-Radiation Missiles (HARM) into battle, allowing it to both jam and eliminate hostile transmitters.

Two lighter attack aircraft joined the A-6 on deck, the F/A-18 Hornet on its first major combat deployment and the A-7, the aircraft it was replacing, on its last. The F/A-18 typically flew with three drop tanks, two AIM-7 and two AIM-9 AAMs, and two HARMs or up to four 1,000lb Mk 83 bombs. HARM-shooting was a key Hornet role.

A VFA-81 F/A-18C flown by Lieutenant Commander Michael 'Spike' Speicher was unlucky enough to be shot down by a surface-to-air missile (SAM), during the initial daylight attacks after the opening night. The mission series included four Hornets hauling 2,000lb Mk 84 bombs to an airfield known as H-3.

Lieutenant Commander Mark Fox and Lieutenant Nick Mongillo were among the four pilots.

In the target area, an E-2 warned them of MiG-21s approaching at 15 miles, head on at Mach 1.2 and with a closing speed of more than 1,200kt. Fox engaged the leader with an AIM-9, following up with an AIM-7, which was engulfed by the fireball of the Sidewinder finding its mark. Mongillo's Sparrow shot destroyed the second MiG. Another Hornet, a

AGM-84E SLAM deployment and every SLAM launch from an A-6E also involved an A-7E.

The only in-theatre A-7 loss affected a VA-72 aircraft that took the barrier on landing after a technical failure. The badly damaged aircraft was stripped of useful parts and then pushed overboard. The last A-7 squadrons returned home to retire their aircraft after 731 Desert Storm sorties and more than 3,100 flying hours.

The Tomcat flew in the fleet defence, air superiority and escort roles for which it had been designed, often remaining close to the attack aircraft in its care. Indeed, the Tomcat's only loss, an F-14B, occurred on January 21 when the aircraft was hit by a SAM during an escort mission against the heavily defended Al Qaim superphosphate fertiliser factory. Standing patrols to counter enemy air activity were therefore allocated to other assets, primarily the USAF F-15 community, which notched up an impressive ❯❯

LEFT: Deck crew added extensive mission markings to several A-7s, including this VA-72 jet. The quantity of GP bombs (unguided bombs), Rockeye (cluster bombs), HARMs and Walleyes expended is recorded, while each camel represents a Desert Storm mission. US Navy

VFA-87 F/A-18A, was shot down on February 5.

At the beginning of Desert Shield, only four A-7E squadrons remained. Among them, VA-37 and VA-105 had wound down almost completely, while VA-46 and VA-72 had relinquished half their Corsair strength while working up on the Hornet. The McDonnell Douglas type had almost but not quite replaced the A-7, leaving USS *John F Kennedy* short of its two light attack squadrons. The ship therefore sailed on August 15, 1990, with newly restored VA-46 and 72 embarked, leaving VA-37 and 105 to continue the business of Hornet conversion.

Veteran thought it was, the A-7 performed magnificently. Serviceability was sufficiently high for large Corsair formations to launch, on occasion almost every jet from both squadrons flew together. Mounting HARMs, the A-7s joined the massive SEAD effort and although they were a

generation behind most of the platforms delivering precision-guided ordnance, they were the only aircraft equipped with the AWW-9 data link pod required by the electro-optically guided AGM-62 Walleye glide bomb. The same pod was a crucial link in

LEFT: The Intruder squadrons typically included a few KA-6D tankers, including this VA-35 jet, flying off USS *Saratoga* during Operation Desert Shield. US Navy

BELOW: This F-14B hailed from VF-103. The unit lost one of its aircraft to a SAM on January 21, 1991. US Navy

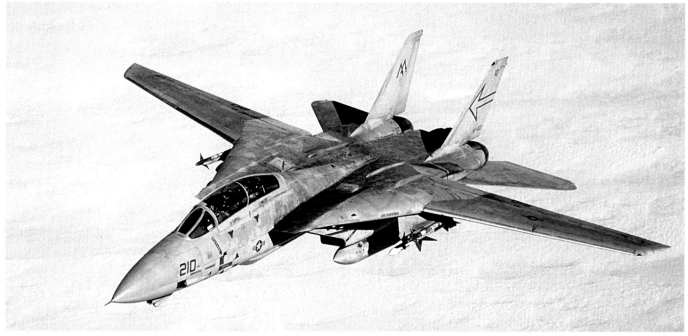

kill tally, while the F-14 returned with just one victory, a Mi-8 helicopter downed on February 6.

Ironically, the Tomcat was perhaps most valuable when employing TARPS to gather pre- and post-strike reconnaissance. It was as a reconnaissance asset that it was ordered back to Al Qaim. Accompanied by two escorting F-14s and with a Prowler jamming, the TARPS aircraft brought back incredibly clear imagery. After the earlier F-14B loss, the three Tomcats exited the target area at Mach 1.2, while the Prowler launched a HARM and continued jamming to cover their egress.

For the US Navy, in common with other Coalition players, Desert Storm saw the widescale employment of precision-guided munitions and

ABOVE: Corsairs, some armed with unguided bombs and others with HARMs, accompanied by a tanker-configured A-6E, refuel from a USAF KC-135E.
US Navy

RIGHT: Taken by a VF-84 F-14A, this photograph demonstrates the spectacular quality delivered by TARPS. It shows two reinforced concrete aircraft shelters on Ahmed Al Jaber airfield, destroyed by Coalition bombing.
US Navy

marked their maturity tactically and technologically compared to the mixed results of Operation El Dorado Canyon. The navy was the only service to launch AGM-84E and AGM-62 missiles, and scored three air-to-air kills, but lost two F/A-18s, four A-6Es and an F-14B.

The war also demonstrated the ability of a single carrier to cover multiple mission types or fly its own fully supported mission package, including command and control, electronic warfare, SEAD, attack, escort, reconnaissance and air-to-air refuelling. Even more significantly, it saw US Navy carrier aircraft operating in mixed strike packages with US Air Force and other Coalition assets.

Desert Storm marked a turning point in military aviation doctrine. In its immediate aftermath the US Navy competed the fleet renewal process begun with the F/A-18 and retired the stalwart A-6. Emphasis was placed on precision ordnance, while greater consideration was given to operations from and over the littoral environment; the US Navy had traditionally expected to meet the Soviet fleet over the deep oceans, in a 'blue water' environment, but future conflict seemed more likely to place carriers offshore while their aircraft fought 'feet dry'.

MCDONNELL DOUGLAS
F/A-18 HORNET

Based on the fallout from a US Air Force lightweight fighter programme that neither service wanted, the F/A-18 ironically became a stalwart of US Navy combat power and will remain a key US Marine Corps platform to 2030.

While the US Navy ordered the F-14 Tomcat to replace the F-4 Phantom II in the fleet defence role, the US Air Force was conducting a similar replacement programme, but with the intention of commissioning an air superiority fighter. While the Tomcat's role was primarily defensive, the USAF wanted an aircraft that could beat allcomers in the air, denying the enemy all opportunity for aerial movement.

The USAF settled upon the McDonnell Douglas F-15 Eagle, developed along a comparable timescale to the F-14 and flying for the first time in 1972. There had been considerable opposition from within the USAF leadership to ordering a

LEFT: The Hornet is of sufficient vintage to have shared carrier deck space with the F-4. Here an F/A-18B awaits launch as a Phantom leaves USS *Kitty Hawk's* waist catapult.
US Navy

larger, more complex jet as the F-4's successor, especially since the US Navy was following a similar route with the F-14.

Concern among military leaders and politicians was such that some USAF officers successfully lobbied for a lighter aircraft. In July 1972 the Department of Defense therefore requested proposals to satisfy its Lightweight Fighter (LWF) programme.

Boeing, General Dynamics, Lockheed, Northrop and Vought submitted proposals, from which the General Dynamics YF-16 and Northrop YF-17 were selected for competitive evaluation. The YF-16 employed a single engine, while the YF-17 used two; both aircraft were of advanced aerodynamic configuration and promised new levels of manoeuvrability.

Still, the USAF majority was reluctant to embrace the LWF, which morphed into the heavier ACF (Air Combat Fighter) project. More paper exercise than hardware requirement, ACF had obvious export potential for operators seeking a next-generation multi-role F-104 Starfighter replacement. The urgency of this requirement pushed ACF along, still based on the YF-16 and YF-17, to reach a conclusion late in 1974. **»**

LEFT: This VMFA-212 F/A-18C was over the South China Sea during its return to Marine Corps Air Station (MCAS) Iwakuni, Japan, after a 2003 exercise in Singapore. Although the Hornet is in the twilight of its USMC career, it remains important to combat strength in the Indo-Pacific region.
US Marine Corps

LEFT: An F/A-18A approaches USS *Constellation* for an arrested landing during operational evaluation in 1983.
US Navy

The lightweight argument had continued to rumble within the US Navy leadership too, and with the F-14 navigating a variety of challenges, in August 1973 Congress launched the VFAX (Navy Fighter Attack Experimental) programme, calling for a multi-role, low cost, lightweight alternative to the Tomcat, in which the US Navy had only passing interest. Realising that the LWF/ACF work might benefit VFAX, Congress subsequently diverted an element of VFAX funding into another new project, the Navy Air Combat Fighter (NACF), designed to absorb LWF/ACF learnings.

Naval twin

Convinced that Congress would push either or both of ACF and NACF into service, General Dynamics and Northrop continued work on their YF-16 and YF-17 designs. General Dynamics teamed with Vought to offer a 'navalised F-16' against NACF, and Northrop recruited McDonnell Douglas to assist in developing a carrier-capable F-17.

On January 13, 1975, the YF-16 was announced as the winning ACF contender, but its single engine was a significant drawback in Navy eyes. The YF-17 therefore had more promise as a carrierborne fighter and was declared winner of the NACF requirement on May 2, 1975. Given its recent experience with the US Navy's F-4 and A-4 Skyhawk, McDonnell Douglas sensibly took the lead on the NACF YF-17, while Northrop agreed to head development of the F-17L land-based version that would compete for exports with the F-16.

The NACF YF-17 now formed the basis of the McDonnell Douglas F/A-18, named 'Hornet' in March 1977 and with a new 'F/A' designation highlighting its equal abilities in the air-to-air and air-to-ground roles. Just as the original LWF concept gained weight on its way to becoming the operationally useful F-16, so the F/A-18 was significantly heavier than the YF-17, while modifications for carrier compatibility also demanded significant reconfiguration. Naval fighters designed for catapult launch and arrested landing (traditionally 'cat and trap' but more recently referred to as CATOBAR, for catapult assisted take off but arrested recovery) are by nature heavier than their land-based equivalents thanks to the reinforced structure, stronger undercarriage and heavier arrester hook demanded by the

HORNET DATA	
F/A-18C	
Length	17.07m (56ft)
Wingspan	11.43m (36ft 6in)
Height	4.66m (15ft 3.5in)
Empty weight	10,455kg (23,050lb)
Maximum take-off weight	22,328kg (49,224lb)
Maximum weapon load	7,711kg (17,000lb)
Maximum speed, more than	1,915km/h (1,190mph)
Climb rate	229m/s (45,000ft/min)
Combat radius, fighter mission, more than	740km (460 miles)
Engines	Two GE F404-GE-400 turbofans each rated at 71.17kN (16,000lb) with afterburner
Armament	One internal 20mm M61A1 Vulcan cannon; typical air-to-air load of two AIM-9 Sidewinder and two AIM-7 Sparrow or AIM-120 AMRAAM AAMs; air-to-ground stores include Mk 80-series unguided bombs, Paveway-series LGBs, Mk 7-series cluster munitions, JDAM and AGM-88 HARM
Total production of all models for all customers	**1,480**

HORNET TIMELINE
First flight F/A-18A Research, Development, Test & Evaluation aircraft – November 18, 1978
First aircraft delivered for training – 1981
First unit conversion – 1982
First cruise began – February 1985
Operation El Dorado Canyon – April 15, 1986
First flight F/A-18C – September 3, 1987
Operation Desert Shield – 1990-91
Operation Desert Storm – 1991
Two Iraqi MiG-21 *Fishbeds* shot down – January 17, 1991
Operation Southern Watch – 1992-2003
Operation Deny Flight – 1993-95
Operation Desert Fox – 1998
Operation Allied Force – 1999
Operation Enduring Freedom – 2001-14
Operation Iraqi Freedom – 2003-10
Operation New Dawn – 2010-11
Operation Inherent Resolve – 2014-present
End of last operational US Navy cruise – March 12, 2018
Final US Navy operational flight – October 2, 2019
Final USMC carrier deployment – 2021
USMC Hornet withdrawal – 2030

US NAVY HORNET VARIANTS
F/A-18A – single-seat Research, Development, Test & Evaluation aircraft, 9 produced, and 371 production aircraft, F404-GE-400 engines
F/A-18A+ – upgrade of F/A-18A to near F/A-18C standard for reserve squadrons
F/A-18A++ – Further upgrade to F/A-18A+ standard

US NAVY HORNET VARIANTS

RF-18A – Second production F/A-18A modified as a reconnaissance aircraft prototype

TF-18A – two-seat RDT&E aircraft based on F/A-18A, 2 produced

F/A-18B – redesignation of TF-18A and production two-seater, 39 produced

F/A-18C – improved avionics and weapons system, F404-GE-402 engine, 137 produced

F/A-18C Night Attack or F/A-18C+ – with AN/APG-73 radar and night attack avionics, 329 produced

F/A-18C+ – new designation for upgraded F/A-18C for USMC Reserve, 19 modified

F/A-18D – two-seater based on F/A-18C, 31 produced

F/A-18D Night Attack or F/A-18D+ – two-seater based on F/A-18C Night Attack, 130 produced

F/A-18D(RC) – Aircraft equipped for the Advanced Tactical Airborne Reconnaissance System (ATARS), 60 modifications

(N)F/A-18C – F/A-18C permanently modified for trials

(N)F/A-18D – F/A-18D permanently modified for trials

air-to-air mission with the F-14, an aircraft that could have been multi-role from the outset but was instead honed around the AWG-9/Phoenix weapons system.

The attack role therefore increasingly fell to the A-4 and A-7 Corsair II squadrons, while the A-6 Intruder shouldered the burden of longer-ranged strikes, but none of these were new platforms. A requirement for a new-generation attack aircraft was clearly emerging and the F/A-18 was well placed to satisfy it.

Unfortunately, the effort to make the Hornet multi-role had created an aircraft that failed to excel in any mission. Although it could manoeuvre hard, the F/A-18 could not match the Tomcat's **»**

RIGHT: Based at Naval Air Station Joint reserve Base Forth Worth, Texas (explaining the Texas flag adorning this colourful F/A-18C), VMFA-112 is subordinate to Marine Aircraft Group 41, part of the 4th Marine Aircraft Wing, a USMC reserve unit. This August 2021 training sortie involved taking fuel from a 155th Air Refueling Wing, USAF KC-135R Stratotanker, an important task in meeting mission readiness requirements.
US Air Force

stresses of repeated 'cat shots' and arrested landings.

Nonetheless, potential export customers noticed McDonnell Douglas' efforts with the F/A-18 and seemed not to care about the compromise it represented as a land-based aircraft. Soon, McDonnell Douglas was actively marketing the Hornet in direct opposition to Northrop and the less developed F-18L, a situation that led the former partners into legal dispute.

Unexpected stopgap
The US Navy had commissioned the F-4 as an air-to-air platform and then adapted it to carry air-to-ground stores with equal ability. It then replaced the Phantom in its

RIGHT: The A-4 Skyhawk was among the types replaced by the F/A-18 in US Navy and Marine Corps service. Here a VMFA-531 F/A-18A leads a VFA-214 A-4M Skyhawk.
US Navy

RIGHT: The Hornet briefly joined the era of 'full-colour' US Navy aircraft markings, prior to April 1985 orders that saw two-tone tactical grey replace the bright markings for so long worn over grey and white on US Navy aircraft. Here an F/A-18A (right) and F-14A sit side-by-side ready to launch.
US Navy

BELOW: The *2022 United States Marine Corps Aviation Plan* stated: "...VMFAT-101 will continue to support aircrew training responsibilities as the only remaining F/A-18 Hornet Fleet Replacement Squadron in the Department of the Navy." It was nevertheless disbanded on September 29, 2023, with responsibility for training Hornet crews passing to VMFA-323. This VMFAT-101 F/A-18D was photographed in 2015.
US Marine Corps

variety of complex USMC missions, including Fast FAC (forward air control delivered from a jet rather than the more traditional observation aircraft) and precision attack. The benefits of its two-crew cockpit have been maximised by 'decoupling', with the forward cockpit focussed on piloting and the rear on weapons system management.

The *2022 United States Marine Corps Aviation Plan* noted the Hornet's final carrier deployment, in 2021, its withdrawal from the US Central Command area of operations and continuing importance in the Indo-Pacific region. It also reported the intention to keep some USMC Hornets flying until 2030, upgrading the best of its existing fleet (around

one third) with AN/APG-74(v4) active electronically scanned array (AESA) radars. Improvements to electronic warfare, weapons and communications systems are also planned.

Smart use of the F/A-18D and upgrades to its A, C and D model Hornets, plus its somewhat different mission set compared to the US Navy, is allowing the USMC to transition from the Hornet, which it describes as a 'bridging platform', to F-35. Before Hornet production ended in 2000, the aircraft had scored export success with Australia, Canada, Finland, Kuwait, Malaysia, Spain and Switzerland. Meanwhile, the US Navy withdrew the F/A-18C from the front line in April 2018.

air-to-air capability, especially against distant targets, and for attack missions it lacked range. Production of the F/A-18A and F/A-18B tandem-two seat trainer nevertheless went ahead, but not until the F/A-18C and D arrived did the Hornet really begin to shine.

Night-attack versions of the 'C' and 'D' quickly replaced the original 'vanilla' specification in production and the night-attack F/A-18D heralded a startling change in Hornet capability. Where the F/A-18B was simply a training aircraft for the Hornet fleet, the F/A-18D was fully missionised for a

NORTHERN WATCH, SOUTHERN WATCH AND DESERT FOX

The legacy of Desert Storm, Operations Northern Watch, Southern Watch and Desert Fox kept the US Navy engaged in southwest Asia into the 2000s.

RIGHT: Lieutenant Carol Watts (in flying kit) discusses her first combat mission with LT Lyndsi Bates after landing back aboard USS Enterprise. Both women flew the F/A-18C with VFA-37. US Navy

After his disastrous invasion of Iran, Saddam Hussein acted against Kurdish settlements in northern Iraq, aiming to eradicate Kurdish rebels supporting his erstwhile enemy. Later, after Desert Storm, Iraqi Kurds and Shias attempted uprisings, again attracting the brutal attention of Hussein's military. Hundreds of thousands of refugees were trapped in the country's north, where lack of food, medicine and shelter claimed thousands of lives.

On April 3, 1991, the UN authorised a relief operation and the US launched Operation Provide Comfort. An airlift of supplies into the region followed, accompanied by combat aircraft administering a no-fly zone that prevented Iraqi interference. The latter gradually became the primary mission and on January 1, 1997, the effort became Operation Northern Watch.

Primarily a USAF mission administered out of Incirlik Air Base, Turkey, Northern Watch also employed USMC and US Navy EA-6B

BELOW: USS Enterprise was solely responsible for the first round of Desert Fox air strikes. US Navy

Prowlers and US Navy Tomcats out of Incirlik, while carrier assets in-theatre were occasionally called upon. The operation ended on March 17, 2003, after the start of Operation Iraqi Freedom.

From August 27, 1992, carrier aircraft were more heavily committed to Operation Southern Watch, instigated in response to UN Security Council Resolution 688, calling for an end to the Iraqi government's repression of its people to the south, especially in Iraqi Kurdistan. The US-led Coalition established a southern no-fly zone, policing it

ABOVE: Engaged in Operation Southern Watch during November 1998, these Prowlers belonged to VAQ-138 in USS *Nimitz* (foreground) and VAQ-137, aboard USS *George Washington*. US Navy

LEFT: Operation Southern Watch continued all hours, as this Hornet launching off USS *Constellation* in the Persian Gulf on July 29, 2001, illustrates. US Navy

ABOVE LEFT: November 17, 2002, and a VAQ-133 EA-6B takes off from Incirlik for an Operation Northern Watch sortie laden with five ALQ-99 jamming pods. US Air Force

with relentless patrols that regularly attracted enemy fire. The response typically came in the form of HARMs fired at the offending radar emitters, plus laser-guided bombs; USAF, US Navy and UK aircraft all engaged in this manner.

The US Navy expended its first Southern Watch weapons on June 29, 1993, when Prowlers fired HARMS. The ebb and flow of low intensity combat continued either side of Operation Desert Fox in 1998, punctuated by an unsuccessful engagement on January 5, 1999, when VF-213 F-14Ds off USS *Carl Vinson* fired two Phoenix at Iraqi MiG-25 *Foxbats*. Southern Watch ended in 2003 as the mission blurred into Operation Iraqi Freedom.

Operation Desert Fox
Operation Southern Watch assets joined other Coalition aircraft for Operation Desert Fox between

December 16 and 19, 1998. The action was in retaliation for Iraq's lack of compliance with US resolutions and its refusal to cooperate with UN Special Commission weapons inspectors seeking evidence of the

country's supposed weapons of mass destruction (WMD).

Desert Fox targets were chosen for their importance to Iraq's WMD capability, but questions remain over its justification. The initial　**»**

LEFT: Allocated to USS *Harry H Truman*, this VF-32 Tomcat was at Incirlik AB, Turkey, for a Northern Watch mission on February 26, 2003. US Air Force

attacks were entirely entrusted to the US Navy, since launching aircraft from USS *Enterprise* was deemed more likely to achieve surprise than from land bases. The navy also fired multiple cruise missiles from surface and subsurface combatants.

First into action were the F-14B Tomcats of VF-32, employing LANTIRN targeting pods to release 1,000lb GBU-12 and 2,000lb GBU-24 laser-guided bombs against air defence targets and debuting the 'Bombcat' in combat. The carrier's Hornets also employed the GBU-24, while its Hawkeyes and Prowlers were busy in their usual mission critical roles. There was also a combat role for the S-3B Viking, which joined US Navy and Marine Corps / F/A-18Cs dropping ADM-141 Tactical Air Launched Decoys (TALD) to further confuse the defenders' air defence radars.

As further assets joined the campaign, USS *Carl Vinson* arrived on station, adding its F-14Ds and more F/A-18Cs to the battle. Desert Fox was considered a success, and the effectiveness of Coalition anti-radar operations led to many SAMs being launched ballistically, ie unguided and in the general direction of the attacking force rather than against a specific target.

As well as marking the Bombcat's debut, Desert Fox is especially notable as the first US Navy combat in which female fast jet pilots were involved. Lieutenant Carol Watts was first away, flying her VFA-37 F/A-18C into action off USS *Enterprise* for the first time on December 17, 1998.

LEFT: VF-211 was deployed for Southern Watch aboard USS *Nimitz* over Christmas 1997. The commanding officer's F-14A was suitably marked for the festivities. Brutus, the squadron emblem, received Santa-themed accessories.
US Navy

LEFT: The Bombcat joined combat for the first time during Operation Desert Fox in 1998. This laser-guided bomb armed VF-31 F-14D was in theatre for Operations Southern Watch and Enduring Freedom in November 2002.
US Navy

BELOW: A VMFA-314 F/A-18 Hornet off USS *Nimitz* refuels from a USAF KC-10 tanker while enforcing the Southern Watch no-fly zone in 1997. US Navy

LEFT: The Royal Navy support tanker HMS *Brambleleaf* comes alongside USS *Kitty Hawk* in the Persian Gulf on May 13, 1999. Both vessels were supporting Operation Southern Watch. US Navy

LEFT: VFA-105 (foreground) and VMFA-312 Hornets prepare to launch for an Operation Desert Fox mission from USS *Enterprise* on December 17, 1998. The navy jet is armed with HARM, the marine aircraft with laser-guided bombs. US Navy

BELOW: USS *Ranger* (CV-61, foreground) and USS *Independence* (CV-62) make an impressive spectacle in this 1993 Operation Southern Watch image. US Navy

DENY FLIGHT, DELIBERATE FORCE AND ALLIED FORCE

Operations Deny Flight, Deliberate Force and Allied Force placed NATO airpower, including carrier aircraft from Italy, Spain, the UK and US, over war-torn Federal Yugoslavia.

O n June 25, 1991, Slovenia emerged as an independent state from Federal Yugoslavia. A brief war with Federal Yugoslav forces followed, ending in a truce, and ultimately a new nation, on July 7. Power in Federal Yugoslavia lay very much with Serbian leader Slobodan Milošević and since Belgrade, the capital of Federal Yugoslavia, was also the capital of the Republic of Serbia, he attempted to enforce his leadership across the Federation.

Milošević responded to Slovenia's declaration by sending armour into the small country, which today borders Italy, Austria, Hungary and Croatia. Fast jet attack aircraft hit Ljubljiana airport in central Slovenia, and positions on the border with Austria and Italy. The well-trained Slovenian Territorial Defence Force, though volunteer manned, soon cut off the Federal supply lines, however, then sat back and awaited

the inevitable surrender. In the end, the European Community brokered a peace deal and from July 7, 1991, Slovenia was independent.

Croatia's recent, complex history led to its own declaration of independence from Federal Yugoslavia, also on June 25, 1991. Its position was complicated by an ethnic Serb population that had claimed autonomy for a region of Croatia and remained loyal to Serbia. Recognising Milošević's hold over the region and the loyalty of Serb nationalist and Federal forces to him, the Croats initially besieged Federal barracks in Croatia. By autumn, sufficient forces had been extracted across the eastern border into Serbia and the long border with Bosnia for the remainder of Federal Yugoslavia, in effect Serbia, to attack Croatia.

Hundreds of thousands of civilians were displaced, such was the ferocity and brutality of the resulting war. On January 15, 1992, the European

Community recognised Croatia as an independent country but the conflict dragged on into August 1995. Croatia had successfully routed the Serbian forces, while many Serbs fled Croatia for another of the Federal Yugoslav republics, Bosnia and Herzegovina, and many others were killed.

Bosnia and Herzegovina was deeply affected by Croatia's and Slovenia's declarations of independence. Its population was divided between Serbs, who wished to remain part of Federal Yugoslavia, and Croats and Bosnian nationals, Bosniaks, who did not. In accordance with their respective loyalties, Bosnia and Herzegovina's political parties attempted to establish

BELOW: It is easy to forget that mundane, necessary tasks continue during operations. Normally based aboard USS *Theodore Roosevelt*, this VAQ-141 Prowler was undergoing a 56-day preventative maintenance inspection.
US Air Force

Croat and Serb regions in defiance of the state government, which declared sovereignty in October 1991 and called a national referendum on independence.

Boycotted by most Serbs, the referendum came out overwhelmingly in favour of independence, which was declared on March 3, 1992; on May 22, the UN accepted the Republic of Bosnia and Herzegovina as a member nation. Almost immediately, Bosnian Serbs rose up in arms alongside Federal Yugoslav army units in Bosnia and Herzegovina. The army withdrew under international pressure, but many of its Serb soldiers simply joined the uprising, forming the so-called Army of the Republic of Serbia. Its brutal drive through the country involved ethnic cleansing, while secondary conflict between Croatians and Bosniaks also involved war crimes.

Flight and Force

The complicated war in Bosnia and Herzegovina ended around 1995, but in summer 1992, NATO had become involved in the wider regional conflict as enforcer of a UN arms embargo on the emerging Balkan republics. A UN No-Fly Zone declared that October had little effect, and NATO fighters therefore deployed under Operation Deny Flight from April 12, 1993. Carrier-based aircraft were involved early in the campaign, with E-2C Hawkeyes initially joining land-based command and control assets.

France, Spain, the UK and US placed aircraft carriers in the Adriatic Sea, bringing multi-role

airpower within easy reach of the conflict zone. France flew aircraft off *Clemenceau*, including the Dassault Etendard IVPM, one of which took a Serbian SAM on April 15, 1994, but returned to the ship safely. The Spanish carrier *Principe de Asturias* operated EAV-8B Harriers, while the UK flew Sea Harriers off HMS *Ark Royal*. The British lost a Sea Harrier to enemy fire the day after the French Etendard had been hit.

On the ground, UN Protection Force (UNPROFOR) troops were coming under increasing threat and in June 1993 it was agreed that NATO aircraft could be used to deliver close air support. The rules of engagement ≫

ABOVE: USS *America* prepares to launch a VA-85 A-6E during Operation Deny Flight. US Navy

LEFT: Although not aircraft carriers in the strictest sense, US Navy amphibious assault ships carry a formidable array of Marine Corps airpower. USS *Nassau* operated AV-8B Harrier II Plus jets and helicopters during Allied Force. These Harriers were returning from a raid on April 14, 1999. Aboard these amphibious assault ships other flying units are considered supporting elements to the lead embarked helicopter (or Osprey today) element, and these Harriers therefore belonged to Helicopter Medium Squadron 266 (HMM-266). US Navy

governing these encounters were complex and restrictive and they became more so in 1994. With the Bosnian capital Sarajevo under siege, UNPROFOR demanded that all artillery pieces around the capital be placed in control points under its protection, with air strikes called against those weapons not surrendered.

Further escalation saw NATO aircraft attacking Serb air defences, before the Serbs twice took UNPROFOR personnel hostage, forcing a reduction in air activity. As spring 1995 turned to summer, activity was again on the increase when Captain Scott O'Grady's F-16 took an SA-6 missile on June 2. The USAF pilot evaded capture until June 8, when a force of US Marines off USS *Kearsarge* rescued him. Two CH-53 helicopters under escort from two AH-1Z gunships and a pair of Harriers swooped in while US Navy Prowlers and USAF EF-111A Ravens jammed Serb transmitters. US Marine Corps F/A-18D, USAF A-10 and Royal Air Force assets were also involved, along with a US Navy SH-60B off USS *Ticonderoga*.

UNPROFOR's attempt to take and hold safe areas was again challenged by Serb hostage taking in July 1995, this latest military and political embarrassment pushing the international community to the brink of wider air attacks. An August 30, a Serb mortar attack on Sarajevo triggered Operation Deliberate Force, a period of powerful airstrikes that continued until September 14, 1995. The US Navy was heavily involved, launching aircraft and cruise missiles. Shocked at the effect of NATO airpower when the cuffs were off, the Bosnian Serbs quickly backed down and the war ended on December 12. By December 20, a

NATO Implementation Force was in command on the ground.

Air activity continued much as it had prior to Deliberate Force, with jets available for close support and monitoring for military activity. In December 1996, the NATO Stabilisation Force (SFOR) replaced IFOR and in December 2004 Operation Althea

began to ensure continuing peace in Bosnia and Herzegovina.

Operation Allied Force

While conflict raged in other Federal Yugoslav republics, the Kosovo region of Serbia witnessed internal disquiet as the Kosovo Liberation Army (KLA) was established in

TOP AND ABOVE: This set of images shows the same VF-84 Tomcat departing for and then recovering from an Operation Deny Flight mission aboard USS *Theodore Roosevelt*. US Navy

LEFT: Equipped with laser-guided bombs and a targeting pod, this F-14 was about to catapult off USS *Theodore Roosevelt* for an Operation Allied Force strike. US Navy

response to the Milošević regime's persecution of ethnic Albanians. Located in southern Serbia, with borders to Montenegro, Albania and North Macedonia, Kosovo saw increasing violence and acts of insurgency through the 1990s.

In February 1998, Kosovan Albanian militias moved against Federal Yugoslav installations in Kosovo, prompting an inevitable response from Serbian forces – Federal Yugoslavia's painful break-up meant that by now it comprised only Serbia and Montenegro. Another war driven by political and ethnic differences broke out and hundreds of thousands of refugees had been displaced from Kosovo by March 1999.

In response to atrocities committed against the Kosovar Albanian population and Federal Yugoslavia's intent to force them from Kosovo, on March 24, 1999, NATO launched Operation Allied Force, a controversial campaign against targets in Serbia that aimed to end Milošević's military capability.

Allied Force struck critical national infrastructure, state broadcasting sites and other strategic military targets in Serbia, including Kosovo itself. Debate over the effectiveness of the bombing and justification for the targets prosecuted continues. It involved warplanes and attack helicopters from across NATO,

LEFT: The US Marine Corps flew out of Aviano Air Base for Operation Allied Force. This VMAQ-2 EA-6B was departing the Italian base for a March 31, 1999, mission. US Air Force

including aircraft launched from USS *Theodore Roosevelt*. US Navy and Marine Corps Prowlers were again instrumental in the jamming and SEAD effort, while F-14s and F/A-18s took on bombing attacks.

Operating alongside their US counterparts, the Aéronavale, the air arm of the French navy, flew the Dassault Super Etendard, in Super Etendard Modernisé (SEM) form, off *Clemenceau*. Italy deployed its aircraft carrier *Giuseppe Garibaldi* and its AV-8B Harriers to the region for combat. As they had been in Operation Deny Flight, Royal Navy Sea Harriers were involved in Allied Force, this time operating off HMS *Invincible*.

An agreement that the UN would oversee Kosovan politics led to a cessation of bombing on June 10, 1999. The war ended on June 12,

by which time Russian, UK and US peacekeepers were in-country. Milošević was tried for war crimes and the end of the Kosovo war signalled an end to his power. In 2009, the Republic of Kosovo was declared an independent state.

US Navy airpower had made a powerful contribution to the Balkan conflicts, unusually while operating alongside the carrier assets of other NATO countries. Once again, the Tomcat had proven its worth as an attack aircraft but the US Navy, in common with other NATO air arms, had relearned the lessons of a previous age – the Federal Yugoslav army had regularly challenged NATO's technological superiority by the simple expedient of camouflage and keeping its forces on the move.

BELOW: Phoenix and Sidewinder missiles, laser-guided bombs and an S-2 Viking share an aircraft elevator aboard USS *Theodore Roosevelt* on April 7, 1999. *Roosevelt* operated in the Adriatic Sea for Operation Allied Force. US Navy

SIKORSKY H-60 SEAHAWK

The cornerstone of US Navy helicopter anti-submarine warfare and surface attack since the late 1980s, the Seahawk began deploying in aircraft carriers from 1989.

Epitomising modern naval helicopter design, Sikorsky's H-60 Seahawk series was not intended for aircraft carrier basing when it was commissioned in September 1977. Under the company designation S-70, Sikorsky was already developing the UH-60 as a replacement for the ubiquitous Bell UH-1 and its proposal for a navalised S-70B was therefore very attractive.

The US Navy wanted a helicopter equipped to provide over-the-horizon targeting and attack capability for a new generation of frigates and destroyers. The SH-60B entered service as such in 1984, equipped for anti-surface and anti-submarine warfare (ASuW and ASW), and secondary roles including search and rescue (SAR) and logistic support. Aside from a large undernose radome for APS-124 search radar, the primary external differences compared to

BOTTOM: This HSM-71 MH-60R was exercising aboard USS *Abraham Lincoln* in the Pacific Ocean on June 7, 2024.

BELOW: Chocks and chains are removed from an SH-60B as it prepares to lift from the Arleigh-Burke class guided-missile destroyer USS *Donald Cook*, deployed to the Mediterranean in December 2016. All US Navy

H-60 DATA	
MH-60R	
Length	19.80m (64ft 10in)
Main rotor diameter	16.40m (53ft 8in)
Height	5.10m (16ft 9in)
Empty weight	6,881kg (15,170lb)
Maximum take-off weight	10,659kg (23,500lb)
Maximum useful load (ASW)	3,003kg (6,620lb)
Cruising speed	252km/h (157mph)
Time on station (ASW)	1.5 hours
Engines	Two GE T700-GE-401C (or -401D) turboshafts each rated at 1,410kW (1,890shp) for take-off
Armament	Two Mk 54 torpedoes, up to four AGM-114 Hellfire AGMs, 70mm APKWS rocket pods, one M60 or M240 machine gun, or GAU-16/A or GAU-17/A Minigun
Production of MH-60R/ MH-60S (with production continuing) more than	900
US NAVY H-60 TIMELINE	
First flight YSH-60B – December 12, 1979	
First flight production SH-60B Seahawk – February 11, 1983	
SH-60B entry into service – 1984	
First SH-60B operational deployment – 1985	
First flight SH-60F – March 19, 1987	
First flight HH-60H – August 17, 1988	
SH-60F entry into service – June 1989	

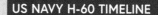

US NAVY H-60 TIMELINE

First HH-60H delivery – July 8, 1989

HH-60H IOC – April 1990

Operation Desert Shield – 1990-91

Operation Desert Storm – 1991

First SH-60F operational deployment – 1991

Operation Desert Fox – 1998

Operation Allied Force – 1999

First flight SH-60B modified to MH-60R standard – December 22, 1999

First flight production MH-60S – January 2000

Operation Enduring Freedom – 2001-14

MH-60S entry into service – February 2002

MH-60S IOC – 2003

Operation Iraqi Freedom – 2003-10

First delivery production MH-60R – August 2005

First MH-60R operational deployment – 2006

Operation New Dawn – 2010-11

Operation Inherent Resolve – 2014-present

HH-60H withdrawn – 2018

Operation Prosperity Guardian – 2023-present

US NAVY H-60 VARIANTS

YSH-60B, T700-GE-401C engines, 5 produced

SH-60B, T700-GE-401C engines, 181 produced for US Navy

SH-60F, carrier-optimised SH-60B variant with dipping sonar

HH-60H, CSAR variant based on SH-60B, 45 produced

MH-60S, combat support helicopter based on SH-60B/UH-60L, 253 in US Navy inventory in 2021

MH-60R, modernised ASW/ASuW variant based on SH-60B, T700-GE-401C/-401D engines, 270 in US Navy inventory in 2021

the UH-60A were that there was a sliding door to the cabin only to starboard and the SH-60B's tailwheel was moved far forward, to reduce its landing footprint aboard ship.

The SH-60 became a permanent fixture aboard carrier decks with the SH-60F, frequently dubbed 'Ocean Hawk', although all US Navy H-60 variants are officially designated Seahawk. Equipped with dipping sonar and taking on the plane-guard role, the SH-60F replaced the legendary SH-3 Sea King in service from June 1989.

A dedicated combat search and rescue (CSAR) helicopter, the HH-60H added elements of the US Coast Guard HH-60J to the SH-60F airframe. Equipped with defensive systems and heavily armed with machine-guns and, optionally, Hellfire missiles, the HH-60H achieved initial operating capability (IOC) in April 1990. After its combat debut in Desert Storm, the HH-60H served extensively in Iraq, frequently alongside US Army and Special Operations Command (SOCOM)

assets. Changes in SOCOM priorities saw the HH-60H withdrawn in 2018.

Meanwhile, a programme to upgrade the original SH-60B capability began in 1993. Lockheed Martin took the lead on a system that effectively integrated modern equivalents of the SH-60B mission and SH-60F dipping sonar avionics suites into the MH-60R, known unofficially as 'Strikehawk' or

'Romeo'. First flown in December 1999, the MH-60R deployed in 2006 and in upgraded form remains the US Navy's primary anti-submarine and combat helicopter, having replaced the SH-60B and SH-60F.

A significant departure from previous US Navy H-60 models, the MH-60S combines the fuselage of the US Army's UH-60L Black Hawk with the naval features of the SH-60B to produce a fleet combat support helicopter. Replacing the CH-46 Sea Knight, the MH-60S is unofficially known as 'Knighthawk'. Commonly deployed in aircraft carriers and other large vessels, the MH-60S achieved IOC in 2003, since when additional equipment has been added to equip it for a variety of additional roles, including mine countermeasures. Significantly, the MH-60R and MH-60S employ Lockheed Martin's Common Cockpit, the first all-glass flightdeck in US Navy service.

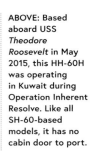

ABOVE: Based aboard USS *Theodore Roosevelt* in May 2015, this HH-60H was operating in Kuwait during Operation Inherent Resolve. Like all SH-60-based models, it has no cabin door to port.

TOP: The dipping sonar installation under the centre fuselage of this SH-60F is evident as it recovers aboard the guided-missile destroyer USS Gonzalez in the Atlantic Ocean in September 2015.

LEFT: An HSC-7 MH-60S lifts from USS *Dwight D. Eisenhower* in the Mediterranean on May 2, 2024. The variant's UH-60L fuselage, including aft tailwheel and sliding doors on both sides of the cabin is obvious.

ENDURING

Launched in response to the 9/11 terrorist attacks, Operation Enduring Freedom saw the US Navy project power far inland, from carriers based in the Arabian Sea.

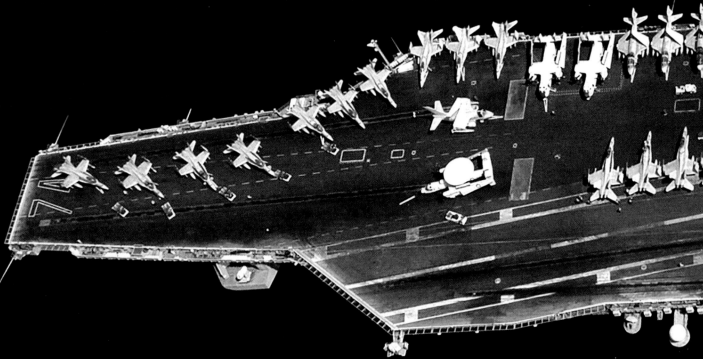

The US Department of Defense instigated Operation Noble Eagle while smoke still rose from the ruined twin towers of the World Trade Center in New York, on September 11, 2001. Noble Eagle has remained the title of operations ensuring US and Canadian homeland security, including the coordination, launch and control of interceptor aircraft.

Primarily a USAF and Royal Canadian Air Force mission, the provision of fighter cover employed US Navy assets briefly in the immediate period after terrorists attacked the World Trade Center and Pentagon with hijacked airliners. San Francisco was covered by F/A-18A Hornets flown by Naval Strike and Air Warfare Center personnel, including instructors from the famous TOPGUN school, out of Naval Air Station Fallon, California.

Responsibility for the terrorist attacks was soon traced to Al-Qaeda, led by Osama Bin Laden and operating under the protection of Afghanistan's Taliban regime. A US-led Coalition was assembled to destroy Al-Qaeda and remove its Taliban sponsors, and on October 7, 2001, Operation Enduring Freedom (OEF) began. With it, the US plunged into a so-called 'War on Terror', which soon merged into a new campaign against Saddam Hussein's Iraq.

The US Navy played a major part in the initial OEF assault, firing cruise missiles and launching long-range precision attacks, primarily with the F-14, which was better able to cover the extended distances from carrier decks in the north Arabian Sea to targets in Afghanistan. In fact, the US Navy employed six carrier battle groups and four amphibious ready groups in the first six months of the campaign and although OEF's initial aims had largely been achieved by December 2001, conflict in Afghanistan rumbled on for two decades.

Carrier war

At its closest, Afghanistan is almost 640km (400 miles) from the sea, meaning a round-trip flight of more than 1,280km (800 miles) for US Navy attack aircraft; in reality, missions were commonly flown to targets almost that far distant, for a 2,560km roundtrip, and once Coalition troops were on the ground, crews regularly orbited for hours, ready to provide close air support on demand.

US Navy aircraft delivered more than 70% of strike missions between October 7 and December 31, 2001, by which time the Taliban had effectively been removed from power. USS *Enterprise* and USS *Carl Vinson* launched the first OEF air strikes, joined by USS *Theodore Roosevelt* from October 15. Some weeks later, USS *John C Stennis* arrived to relieve *Enterprise*, which had been away from its home port for seven months. USS *Kitty Hawk*, meanwhile, sailed from Japan to act as a forward »

ABOVE: USS *John C Stennis* joined Operation Enduring Freedom after it was a few weeks old. This later image shows it in the north Arabian Sea with Greyhounds, Hawkeyes, Hornets, Prowlers, Seahawks, Super Hornets and Vikings spotted on deck. US Navy

FREEDOM

RIGHT: The US DoD coined the term 'maritime security operations' to cover deployments in southwest Asia, where naval assets in the Persian Gulf and Arabian Sea carried out Operation Enduring Freedom and, from 2003, Iraqi Freedom missions. This F-14D was approaching to recover aboard USS *Theodore Roosevelt* during a maritime security deployment in the Persian Gulf on January 6, 2006.
US Navy

staging post for special forces missions. The carrier air wings averaged 30-40 daily missions, some lasting as long as ten hours, with inflight refuelling from USAF and Coalition tankers.

Once again, the Prowler proved its worth jamming radar and communications. F-14s and F/A-18s were busy flying attack missions and approximately 93% of the munitions they expended were precision-guided; around 84% of these are believed to have exactly found their mark. These weapons included the GPS-guided 2,000lb GBU-31 Joint Direct Attack Munition (JDAM), 1,000lb GBU-16 Paveway laser-guided bomb, AGM-65 Maverick and AGM-84 Standoff Land Attack Missile-Extended Range (SLAM-ER).

During the campaign's first ten days, attacks were primarily against fixed military infrastructure targets, switching to moving and fleeting targets as al-Qaeda and Taliban personnel began moving away from the areas under attack. Laser designation was often from forward controllers on the ground, and sometimes applied to weapons released against precise coordinates rather than the laser 'sparkle' itself.

Close air support

With an interim Afghan government in place, Al-Qaeda and Taliban forces hid in the Tora Bora caves of eastern Afghanistan. A Coalition ground campaign in the region during December 2001 relied on air support, much of it from the US Navy. The same was true of

LEFT: Colourfully marked as Carrier Air Wing 14's 'CAG-bird', this VFA-113 F/A-18C Hornet was over southern Afghanistan on July 7, 2009. Flying off USS *Ronald Reagan*, the aircraft carriers a JDAM under its starboard wing and a laser-guided Paveway bomb to port. US Navy

LEFT: USS *Abraham Lincoln* was engaged in Operation Enduring Freedom, Iraqi Freedom and other missions during this 2008 deployment to the north Arabian Sea. This VFA-137 F/A-18E was being prepared for a mission on July 8. US Navy

LEFT: The permissive air environment over Afghanistan enabled tankers to orbit overhead while tactical aircraft came up for regular top-offs. Here a US Navy F/A-18C, loaded with laser-guided bombs, refuels from a USAF KC-10 Extender. US Navy

Operation Anaconda in March 2002, in which the Coalition fought to take control of the strategically important Shah-i-Kot Valley and surrounding mountains, through which Al-Qaeda and Taliban insurgents were thought to be gaining access to Pakistan.

The US Marine Corps had played an important role in the success to date, including launching an airborne amphibious assault from USS *Peleliu* and USS *Bataan* over 740km into Afghanistan, where Forward Operating Base Rhino was established and effectively prevented residual Taliban forces in the north joining with those to the south. Rhino also served as a staging point to Kandahar Airfield, which was quickly prepared to support Coalition assets.

On November 21, 2001, France deployed *Charles de Gaulle* and its Super Etendard SEM jets to the region under Mission Héraclès. From March 2, 2002, the SEMs were heavily committed to supporting Operation Anaconda, working closely with French and other troops on the ground. When the Rafale M joined combat, the SEM deployed several more times to designate targets for the new jet's laser-guided bombs.

Rafale M first deployed for Enduring Freedom in 2002. The aircraft was to F1 standard, without air-to-ground capability and with no airborne threat over Afghanistan its usefulness was limited. Training off *Charles de Gaulle* in the Gulf of Oman was completed, however, and patrols flown over the India/Pakistan border after the carrier moved into the Arabian Sea in June. Later, the Rafale M redeployed as a 'bomb truck', releasing weapons against targets designated for it by the Super Etendard SEM.

ABOVE: USS *Dwight D Eisenhower* launches a VFA-83 F/A-18C during maritime security operations in 2016, after Operation Enduring Freedom had become Operation Freedom's Sentinel. US Navy

LEFT: July 10, 2008, and USS *Abraham Lincoln* launches a VFA-2 F/A-18F in the north Arabian Sea. The aircraft is armed with a Maverick missile to starboard and JDAM to port. *Lincoln* was engaged in Operations Enduring Freedom and Iraqi Freedom. US Navy

Although not exclusively involving aircraft carriers, since Iraqi's August 1990 invasion of Kuwait, the US Navy had also performed maritime interception operations (MIO) in the Arabian Sea, Gulf of Oman and Persian Gulf. Any suspicious vessels were intercepted, boarded and searched. Now it seemed likely that senior Al-Qaeda and Taliban leaders might attempt their escape through Pakistan and onward by boat, and MIO gained new significance as it became leadership interdiction operations (LIO). »

RIGHT: USS *Enterprise* was among the first carriers to launch Operation Enduring Freedom missions, although this F/A-18F 'cat shot' was in 2006. The Super Hornet was heading for Afghanistan and another close air support mission. US Navy

LEFT: With
Paveway bombs
in the foreground,
aviation
ordnancemen
use 'bomb skids'
to move 500lb
GBU-38 weapons
aboard USS
Harry S Truman.
US Navy

BELOW: On
October 25,
2001, when this
photograph was
taken, Enduring
Freedom was still
a neo operation.
This F/A-18C was
refuelling from a
USAF KC-135R, the
empty pylon under
its starboard wing
suggesting that
some ordnance
has already
been expended.
US Air Force

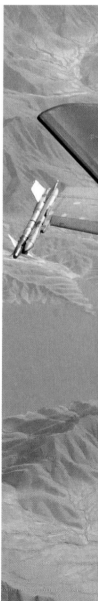

It also expanded geographically, with air support; on November 23, 2001, for example, USS *Princeton* and aircraft off USS *Theodore Roosevelt* performed some of the first LIO missions as far away as Gwadar, off southwestern Pakistan. Sometimes vessels failed to comply with Coalition intercepts, as was the case with an early December 2001 MIO when *Roosevelt* launched an HH-60H and SH-60F to assist in the stop and search of M/V *Kota Sejarah* off Karachi, Pakistan.

Mission failed

Back in Afghanistan, the Taliban had effectively melted away into the country's rugged landscape. Through the summer of 2002 they avoided destruction and began the process of regrouping before embarking on a campaign of insurgency that continued until a major Coalition operation attempted to counter it in May 2006.

A period of complex political and military manoeuvring followed in which the Coalition attempted to hand control of Afghanistan back to a democratically elected government. After years of reconstruction and training, control was largely transferred from December 31, 2014, when Operation Enduring Freedom ended; on January 1, 2015, Operation Freedom's Sentinel began as a lower level involvement within the wider context of the Global War on Terror.

Foreign powers have been attempting and failing to bend Afghanistan to their will for generations and the Coalition effort ultimately failed too. Control was passed back to the Taliban in 2020 and on August 31, 2021, the last US personnel left Kabul.

Two decades of costly operations in Afghanistan ultimately achieved little. The US Navy became less involved as in-country land bases opened, but in the operation's early and most successful stages, it had employed aircraft carriers in a new way. Never before had they launched aircraft so far inland to strike a distant enemy with precision and persistence.

ABOVE: An HSM-71 MH-60R Seahawk is cleared to lift from USS *John C Stennis* on January 8, 2012. The ship was in the Arabian Sea on Enduring Freedom duty.
US Navy

BOEING F/A-18 SUPER HORNET AND EA-18G GROWLER

The Super Hornet is and will remain for some years the cornerstone of US Navy fighter and attack capability. The Growler brings advanced jamming and electronic attack options to the fleet.

RIGHT: The first F/A-18F approaches to land aboard the US Navy's then newest aircraft carrier, USS *John C Stennis*, during the type's initial sea trials in January 1997.
All US Navy

BELOW: A VFA-137 F/A-18E lands back aboard USS *Nimitz*, sailing in the Pacific in July 2024.

There is a certain irony in the fact that the US Navy relies on the F/A-18E and F Super Hornet as the core of its carrierborne airpower. Significantly larger and more capable than its legacy Hornet forebear, the Super Hornet nonetheless grew from a design the Navy originally did not want. Significant upgrades have enabled the Super Hornet to keep pace with the latest avionics and weapons developments, while its frontline use in single- and two-seat forms introduced the US Navy to new tactics. Furthermore, the F/A-18F has been developed into the EA-18G electronic attack and jamming platform.

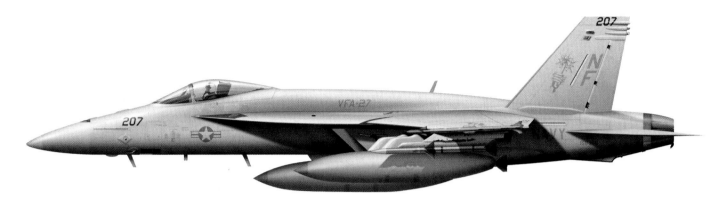

LEFT: A VFA-22 F/A-18F launches from USS *Ronald Reagan* in July 2009. The ship was underway in the Arabian Sea, a common operating location for the Super Hornet.

BELOW: A cluster of Super Hornets, spotted on the deck of USS *Nimitz*, serves to illustrate the different cockpit arrangements of the F/A-18E (foreground) and F/A-18F.

While it reluctantly took the F/A-18 Hornet and gradually refined it into a fitting replacement for the A-4 Skyhawk and A-7 Corsair II, the US Navy worked to add attack capability and replace its earlier A-6 Intruder models with the new A-6F, upgraded F-14D and all-new, stealthy McDonnell Douglas/General Dynamics A-12. The legacy Hornet, in upgraded form, was also considered as a potential supplement to the A-12.

The end of the Tomcat's US Navy service was already looming when the F-14D appeared and although it was a capable platform, relatively few entered service. The idea of further improvements to the Intruder was ultimately abandoned in favour of the A-12 as budgets were reduced before, in 1991, the A-12 fell by the wayside too. An attack aircraft beyond the A-12, known initially as AX and later as A/F-X, had been simultaneously »

under study for service from 2020, but in the meantime a stopgap between A-6E and AX was required.

Commissioning more F-14Ds was one solution. Another was to further develop the Hornet, which had begun to show its mettle as the F/A-18C. With luck, this next-generation Hornet could take over the long-range attack role of the A-6E and F-14D and replace the F-14 variants flying fleet defence. In June 1992, therefore, McDonnell Douglas received an order for five single-seat F/A-18E and two dual-seat F/A-18F Engineering & Manufacturing Development (EMD) aircraft. The new type was named Super Hornet.

The importance of weight

On November 9, 1989, the Berlin Wall fell. The USSR was formally dissolved a little over two years later, by which time Germany had been reunified. The Cold War was over and Western governments were quick to cash in on the so-called peace dividend. Defence budgets were slashed as the perceived threat receded and A/F-X was cancelled. The Super Hornet was now the US Navy's only option for covering even more mission sets, including the air-to-air tanker role latterly adopted by the S-3B Viking and the specialist electronic attack role built around the EA-6B Prowler, while the multi-role F/A-18C would also need a replacing. These added to the long-range attack and fleet defence requirements, albeit the Super Hornet would lack the Tomcat's reach, since a planned new long-range missile to replace Phoenix had also been cancelled.

Weight was a critical parameter for the Super Hornet design team. To match the Intruder's range the aircraft needed to carry more fuel than the Hornet, adding fuel and structural weight to the airframe. It also needed to be able to return to the carrier carrying a considerable ordnance load.

The Intruder had been designed as a 'bomb truck', hauling large loads of unguided ordnance released using the most advanced targeting systems of the day, but lacking the precision strike capability of the laser-guided weapons proven during Desert Storm or the emerging promise of GPS guidance. Precision-guided munitions (PGM) had the advantages of requiring fewer weapons and aircraft to successfully prosecute a target, while minimising the risk of collateral damage to civilians and infrastructure.

But precision comes at a price and with laser-guided bombs costing orders of magnitude more than their 'dumb' equivalents, dropping

SUPER HORNET DATA

F/A-18E

Length	18.50m (60ft 3.5in)
Wingspan	13.68m (44ft 8.5in)
Height	4.87m (16ft)
Empty weight	14,552kg (32,100lb)
Maximum take-off weight	29,937kg (66,000lb)
Maximum weapon load	8,050kg (17,750lb)
Maximum speed	Mach 1.6
Climb rate	229m/s (45,000ft/min)
Combat radius, attack mission, approximately	1,223km (760 miles)
Engines	Two GE F414-GE-400 turbofans each rated at 97.86kN (22,000lb) with afterburner
Armament	One internal 20mm M61A1/A2 Vulcan cannon; AIM-9 Sidewinder and AIM-120 AMRAAM AAMs; air-to-ground stores include AGM-84 Harpoon, AGM-84E SLAM, AGM-84H/K SLAM-ER, AGM-154 JSOW, Paveway-series LGBs, JDAM and AGM-88 HARM
US Navy production (projected by 2027)	698

SUPER HORNET/GROWLER TIMELINE

First flight F/A-18E EMD – November 29, 1995	
First flight F/A-18F EMD – April 1, 1996	
F/A-18E Block I service entry – 1999	
Operation Southern Watch – 2002-03	
First combat mission – November 6, 2002	
First flight F/A-18F modified as EA-18G Growler – November 2003	
Start of F/A-18E/F Block II production – 2005	
First flight EA-18G Growler prototype – 2006	
Operation Enduring Freedom – 2001-14	
Operation Iraqi Freedom – 2003-10	
First production EA-18G delivery – 2008	
Operation New Dawn – 2010-11	
First EA-18G combat mission – 2011	
Operation Inherent Resolve – 2014-present	
Syrian Su-22 *Fitter* shot down – June 18, 2017	
Last US Navy F/A-18E/F Block II delivery – April 2020	
First flight F/A-18E/F Block III – May 2020	
First US Navy F/A-18E/F Block III delivery – 2021	
Operation Prosperity Guardian – 2023-present	
Expected end of production – 2027	

SUPER HORNET/GROWLER VARIANTS

F/A-18E EMD – single-seat aircraft, F414-GE-400 engines, AN/APG-73 radar, 5 produced
F/A-18E Block I – stopgap initial production model, similar avionics to F/A-18C
F/A-18E Block II – primary production standard, AN/APG-79 AESA radar, improved avionics and weapons system, some new production, some Block I upgrades, 322 Block I/II produced
F/A-18E Block III – further improved avionics and weapons system, including IRST, many Block II upgrades planned
F/A-18F EMD – two-seat EMD aircraft. F414-GE-400 engines, AN/APG-73 radar, 2 produced
F/A-18F Block I – stopgap initial production two-seat model

SUPER HORNET/GROWLER VARIANTS

F/A-18F Block II – primary production standard, AN/APG-79 AESA radar, improved avionics and weapons system, some new production, some Block I upgrades, 286 Block I/II produced

F/A-18E/F Block III – final production standard, potential upgrade of more than 400 F/A-18E/F Block II, up to 95 produced new by 2027

EA-18G Growler – jamming/electronic attack aircraft based on F/A-18F Block II, AN/APG-79 radar and mission avionics, 1 conversion and 160 produced

unexpended ordnance into the sea to bring an aircraft down to safe carrier landing weight was no longer an easy option. The Super Hornet therefore needed not only to carry more payload than the Hornet, but it also needed to be able to bring more of it back to the carrier.

The Super Hornet's superior bring-back capability was achieved by enlarging its wing area, with a resultant increase in thickness to retain structural strength. This inevitably increased drag and the leading edge was more sharply swept in compensation. Without further modification, this would have left the new jet inferior to the old one at low speeds and in air-to-air combat, so the leading edge root extensions (LERX) were enlarged. A longer fuselage made space for more fuel and future avionics, while »

RIGHT: Flying an Inherent Resolve sortie in March 2016, this Growler (leading) and F/A-18E provide an interesting comparison between Super Hornet variants.

BELOW: A pair of VAQ-139 Growlers leads a brace of US Marine Corps F/A-18C Hornets during Operation Inherent Resolve, in September 2020. Both VAQ-139 and VMFA-323, the Hornet unit, were based in USS *Nimitz*.

ABOVE: Wearing colourful markings as VFA-22's 'CAG-bird', this F/A-18F was flying off USS *Nimitz* in July 2024.

engineering provision was made in advance for their electrical supply.

The resulting aircraft was inevitably larger than the Hornet and weighed 25% more. General Electric's F414 turbofan, a more powerful evolution of the Hornet's F404 was chosen to power it, sitting behind enlarged, reshaped intakes. Oddly, when a Super Hornet is parked alongside a Hornet the differences are obvious, but in isolation, the most foolproof means of recognising a Super Hornet is by these large, 'square' intakes.

The EMD programme was well under way when Boeing and McDonnell Douglas merged on August 1, 1997. Work continued under the Boeing brand to deliver an initial production standard that offered operational capability similar to that of the latest F/A-18C standard, with APG-73 radar. The F/A-18E/F could lift more and fly further, but the

F414 proved a little underpowered for the aircraft and the F/A-18C remained markedly superior in air-to-air combat.

Like the legacy model before it, the Super Hornet showed great promise, however, and 222 aircraft were ordered in 2000. The type deployed for the first time in 2002, ready for Operation Southern Watch.

Later production examples of the so-called Block I aircraft were

LEFT: Loaded with an asymmetric load of laser- and GPS-guided munitions, plus a Maverick missile, targeting pod and two drop tanks, this VFA-11 F/A-18F was launching for a December 2007 mission off USS *Harry S Truman* in the Persian Gulf.

RIGHT: The Super Hornet took over the carrierborne tanker role latterly held by the S-3B and previously by the KA-6D Intruder. Here an F/A-18F refuels an F/A-18E in a September 2004 demonstration.

ABOVE: Enlarged leading edge root extensions ensured the Super Hornet retained impressive high angle-of-attack performance. Here vapour is forming in vortices at the LERX leading edges as a VFA-27 F/A-18E pilot pulls g.

compatible with the AN/ASQ-228 Advanced Targeting Forward-Looking Infrared (ATFLIR) pod, featured the MIDS (Multifunctional Information Distribution System) data link, and boasted greater processing power and new cockpit displays.

Growler

The forward fuselages of the early F/A-18E/F production aircraft were like those of the Hornet, but a complete redesign prepared the Block II Super Hornet for improved systems. Designed for a new cockpit and radar, the structure was

introduced from 2003. Seemingly unchanged from the outside, it comprised fewer parts, making it easier to build and maintain.

Compared to the late production Block I, Block II introduced the AN/APG-79 active electronically scanned array (AESA) radar. This powerful unit adding jamming functionality and the opportunity for an F/A-18F crew to employ different radar modes simultaneously.

With the AN/APG-79 capable of jamming, the Block II Super Hornet already had the makings of an EA-6B replacement. Indeed, such is the commonality between the F/A-18F

and EA-18G Growler that an F/A-18F may have evolved into a Growler on the production line if required, the two models diverging quite late in the build process.

The F/A-18F was chosen because the US Navy considers the high-workload electronic attack mission a two-crew task. In addition to the standard AN/APG-79 radar, the EA-18G employs a modernised version of the Prowler's podded AN/ALQ-99 tactical jamming system; as many as five pods may be carried, but two or three is typical. The AGM-88 High-speed Anti-Radiation Missile (HARM) is carried for electronic ❯❯

BELOW:
In combination,
the F-35C (leading)
and Super Hornet
(F/A-18E, in trail)
deliver unique
capability. These
aircraft were
working together
during Exercise
Rim of the Pacific
(RIMPAC) 2024.

attack when the mission requires that emitters stay off air. The Growler may also jam communications and gather electronic intelligence, while still transmitting data securely.

An F/A-18F modified to represent the EA-18G first flew in November 2003. The Growler programme was complex, and it was early 2008 before the initial production aircraft was delivered; the EA-18G joined combat in 2011, supporting NATO operations over Libya.

Although Growler production ended in 2020 along with the Block II upon which it is based, the type is subject to upgrade. Most significantly, AN/ALQ-249 is replacing AN/ALQ-99. Equipped with an AESA and open systems architecture, the new system was delivered for trials in July 2022 and the US Navy received its first production example in July 2023.

Meanwhile, from 2007, new weapons were added to the Block II, the AIM-120D, offering 50% more range than the AIM-120C-7, and AIM-9X among them. More weapons, cockpit improvements and an infrared search and track (IRST) system were subsequently added. The IRST, installed in the nose of a centreline drop tank, required no aircraft structural modifications, while mission software changes 'fused' IRST, radar and other data into a coherent 'picture' for the crew.

Final block

Production switched to the Block III in 2020. Boeing had schemed an aircraft equipped with conformal overwing fuel tanks, a stealthy munitions pod, new avionics and cockpit revisions, plus a built-in IRST, with power from the F414 Enhanced Performance Engine (EPE), which produced more thrust while burning less fuel. The configuration the US Navy purchased in 2017 was somewhat downgraded but led to first deliveries in 2021. The navy originally ordered 78 jets, then reduced its ambition, but more were added in batches, including a final five F/A-18E and 12 F/A-18F jets for delivery no later than spring 2027. Some 420 Growler and Super Hornet aircraft were in US Navy service at the beginning of 2024 and upgrade work is expected to continue into the 2030s.

The successor to the Hornet, the jet the US Navy did not originally want, the Super Hornet is likely to serve for more than two decades alongside the Lockheed Martin F-35C Lightning II, into the 2040s. There are operational benefits to be had in some mission scenarios where the 4th- or even 4.5th-generation F/A-18E/F and F-35 work together. Those lessons are still being learned and in that context, Super Hornet capability is likely to continue expanding right up until the type's withdrawal, as much as seven decades after the F/A-18A entered service.

IRAQI
FREEDOM AND NEW DAWN

Operation Iraqi Freedom called on US Navy aircraft carriers to launch parallel combat efforts over Iraq and Afghanistan.

On March 20, 2003, the War on Terror spread to Iraq, when a US-led Coalition launched Operation Iraqi Freedom (OIF). The war was justified politically as a response to Iraq's continuing non-compliance with UN weapons inspectors seeking evidence for weapons of mass destruction, while US President George W Bush had already identified the country as a component in what he termed the 'Axis of Evil'. There appears to

be little or no evidence for Iraq's involvement in state-sponsored terrorism and it may never have been close to producing weapons of mass destruction, but further discussion is beyond the scope of this narrative.

Like Operation Enduring Freedom, OIF was fought in a permissive air environment, where ground based air defences rather than enemy aircraft were the major threat to air operations. The complex and shifting situation on the ground

caused crews, including those of the US Navy and Marine Corps already engaged in OEF from the same aircraft carriers, to develop new tactics for the safe delivery of precision-guided weapons close to friendly troops.

Long before it began at 05:34hrs local time on March 20, 2003, OIF's aim was the invasion of Iraq and removal of Saddam Hussein as its leader. The powerful invasion force took Baghdad on April 9, signalling an end to Hussein's rule. President ››

BELOW: Late in December 2004, personnel aboard USS *Harry S Truman* position a VF-32 F-14B for launch on an intelligence, surveillance and reconnaissance (ISR) mission over Iraq. US Navy

USS *John C Stennis* was deployed to the north Arabian Sea for maritime security operations in 2006. Much of its work therefore revolved around OEF and OIF.
US Navy

ABOVE: A VAQ-130 Prowler sits alongside F/A-18s aboard USS *Harry S Truman*, in the Persian Gulf on December 20, 2004. US Navy

RIGHT: Even in the early stages of OIF – this photograph was taken on April 11, 2003 – there was no air-to-air threat to Coalition aircraft over northern Iraq, rendering this Tomcat's AIM-9 AAMs irrelevant. The Paveway under its fuselage tells a different story however, about providing close air support over a complex battlefield. The jet was up from USS *Harry S Truman*. US Navy

Bush chose USS *Abraham Lincoln* as the platform from which to announce the end of OIF's major combat phase on May 1, yet Iraq's brutal former leader remained at large until December 13, when he was captured.

On November 5, 2006, Hussein was found guilty of crimes against humanity and on December 30 he was hanged. A bitter insurgency across Iraq had marked the period between the fall of Baghdad and end of 2006 and those Coalition leaders who thought Hussein's death might end it were disappointed.

War against insurgency

The Coalition initially upped its use of airpower towards the end of 2003 as the insurgency gained momentum, and on March 31, 2004, a US military contractor convoy was attacked in the city of Fallujah; US forces responded with an attack on the city, an effort repeated in November. Elsewhere in Iraq, the so-called New Iraqi Army was standing up with assistance from US advisors.

Regular insurgent attacks continued, punctuated by an occasional larger effort, including the Battle of Abu Ghraib, in April 2005. In December, the Iraqi National Assembly was elected but hopes for a new, democratic future were dashed by atrocities committed by combatants on both sides. The conflict also gained a new aspect in February, after a mosque was bombed, possibly by Al-Qaeda. A new Iraqi government took office on May 20 and the US tracked and eliminated Al-Qaeda's leader in Iraq on June 6, while the UN declared that Iraq was effectively experiencing civil war, since the insurgency was increasingly targeting Iraqi security personnel.

During 2007, the Iraqi government first requested a schedule for the withdrawal of overseas forces as Coalition support for the war

waned, yet the US committed more troops. The situation in Iraq became even more complex as a variety of organisations took advantage of the civil war to train and equip militias for their own purposes.

In December 2008, the US and Iraq agreed that all US forces would leave the country by December 31, 2011. In February 2009, President Barack Obama declared that US troops would disengage from combat by August 31, 2010, albeit leaving a large force responsible for training Iraqi personnel. The UK ended its operations on April 10 and on June 29, US troops exited Baghdad. Australia withdrew on July 28.

The Iraqi military was left facing an increasingly bold insurgency, while the country's government was in turmoil. On September 1, 2010, Operation Iraqi Freedom became **»**

ABOVE: The Prowler and Hawkeye provided stalwart support to carrier aviation for decades. Here a VAQ-138 EA-6B approaches to land aboard USS *John C Stennis* in 2005, while a crewman awaits alongside a colourful Hawkeye. US Navy

BELOW: The Tomcat saw out its US Navy career in Operations Enduring Freedom and Iraqi Freedom. This F-14D was in combat over Iraq in 2004. US Navy

Operation New Dawn, under which the first US 'Advise and Assist' unit arrived in theatre on the 8th. New Dawn witnessed the worst month in Iraq for US deaths since 2003, when 15 service personnel were killed in June 2010. Ultimately, all US troops were withdrawn and the mission in Iraq is considered to have ended on December 15, 2011.

Iraq was left lawless. With an ineffective government. Civil unrest continued largely unchecked, the security situation providing an ideal background against which new terrorist organisations trained and equipped, the Islamic State in Iraq and the Levant (ISIL, later known simply as IS, and now as Islamic State of Iraq and Syria, ISIS) among them.

In June 2014, ISIL took Mosul and Tikrit, Iraqi Kurds held key positions in Kirkuk, and Al-Qaida designated Iraqi territory under its control as a new state. Iraqi security forces failed to respond effectively to these new threats and in September 2014 President Obama authorised the use of US aircraft in support. Once again the US Navy's aircraft carriers, which had operated throughout the eight-year long conflict in Iraq, were called back into action.

Powerful support from US combat aircraft continued as war raged between ISIL and the Iraqi government, the US also supporting individual groups fighting ISIL, the common enemy. The latter had taken Raqqa as its capital, and after this fell to Kurdish troops in 2017, ISIL fell into decline; the Iraqi government declared ISIL

LEFT: Although they did not operate from carriers, US Marine Corps Hornets saw considerable combat over Iraq. These VMFA(AW)-121 F/A-18Ds were taxiing for a mission from Al Anbar, Iraq in April 2007.
US Marine Corps

defeated in December and through 2018, insurgency in Iraq calmed.

US personnel had never entirely left Iraq. Around 5,000 had remained in support of the US embassy and other functions. In January 2020 the Iraqi government demanded their withdrawal, but after US President Donald Trump threatened sanctions they were allowed to remain; in 2023 it was agreed that Iraq would host an indefinite US military presence.

Operation New Dawn and the subsequent uptick in US military air support to allied forces over Iraq effectively blurred into Operation Inherent Resolve, an international campaign to destroy ISIS. That operation continued at the time of writing in summer 2024 and, as they have since 2001, US Navy carriers in the region continue to deploy airpower against an elusive, complicated and fluid terrorist threat.

BELOW: USS *Harry S Truman* begins a journey through the Suez Canal on January 5, 2003. The Prowlers and Hornets arrayed on its flight deck would soon be flying OIF combat.
US Navy

SUKHOI SU-33 FLANKER-D

Emerging just as the Cold War thawed, the Su-33 has been hampered in service by issues with Russia's only aircraft carrier.

Analogous to the McDonnell Douglas F-15 Eagle and of roughly similar vintage, the Sukhoi Su-27 began entering service in the mid-1980s. Given the Air Standards Coordination Committee codename (sometimes referred to as NATO codename) *Flanker*, the Su-27 left Western observers impressed and concerned by its demonstrations of extreme manoeuvrability and apparently advanced radar and missile systems.

Designed in an era when the Cold War was chilliest, the Su-27 appeared in service just as the beginnings of a thaw became apparent, and budgetary constraints curtailed its early development somewhat. Funding difficulties and the changing political climate also curtailed the Soviet Union's plans for a new aircraft carrier fleet to replace its old Kiev-class vessels. Operating the Yakovlev Yak-38 *Forger*,

these ships were always compromised by the V/STOL fighter's complexity and limited capability. In the event, the new Admiral Kuznetsov-class produced only one ship for the Russian Navy, while the larger Ulyanovsk-class produced only scrap.

Nonetheless, naval variants of several Soviet combat aircraft were schemed, among them the Su-27,

which was considered as the basis for a fleet defender operating alongside a fighter/attack MiG-29. Initially designated Su-27K, the carrierborne Su-27 featured canard foreplanes from the outset for reduce landing approach speeds, plus reinforced undercarriage, arrester hook, ailerons, revised flaps and an inflight refuelling probe.

LEFT: Su-33 'Red 88' shows off the type's foreplanes and arrester hook. Igor Bubin/ WikimediaCommons

BELOW: Su-33 'Red 78' has wing tip Sorbitsiya electronic support measures pods. Dmitry Terekhov/ WikimediaCommons

SU-33 DATA		J-15 DATA	
Length	21.19m (69ft 6in)	Length	22.28m (73ft 1in)
Wingspan	14.70mm (48ft 3in)	Wingspan	15m (49ft 3in)
Height	5.93m (19ft 5in)	Height	5.92m (19ft 5in)
Empty weight	18,400kg (40,565lb)	Empty weight	17,500kg (38,581lb)
Maximum take-off weight	33,000kg (75,753lb)	Maximum take-off weight	32,500kg (71,650lb)
Maximum weapon load	6,500kg (14,330lb)	Maximum weapon load	6,500kg (14,330lb)
Maximum speed, more than	2,300km/h (1,400mph)	Maximum speed	Mach 2.4
Climb rate	246m/s (48,400ft/min)	Ferry range	3,500km (2,200 miles)
Range	3,000km (1,900 miles)	Engines	Two AL-31 turbofans each rated at 122.60kN (27,600lb) with afterburner or two WS-10B turbofans each rated at 135kN (30,000lb) with afterburner
Engines	Two AL-31F3 turbofans each rated at 125.50kN (28,200lb) with afterburner	Armament	One internal 30mm GSh-30-1 cannon; PL-8, PL-10, PL-12 and PL-15 AAMs; YJ-83K AShM; YJ-91 ARM; KD-88 AGM; various guided and unguided bombs
Armament	One internal 30mm GSh-30-1 cannon; R-27 and R-73 AAMs; S-8, S-13 and S-25 rockets; Kh-31 and Kh-41 AShMs; Kh-25 and Kh-31 ARMs; various guided and unguided bombs	Production (may remain in production)	60
Production	24		

SU-33/J-15 TIMELINE

First flight Su-27K – August 17, 1987

Su-27K achieves first arrested landing on a Russian carrier – November 1, 1989

Su-27K cruise – December 1995-March 1996

Service entry Su-33 – 1998

First flight two-seat Su-27KUB – April 1999

First flight J-15 prototype – August 31, 2009

First flight upgraded Su-33 – October 2010

First flight two-seat J-15S – November 4, 2012

First J-15 carrier operations – November 25, 2012

J-15T flight test began – 2016

Further Su-33 upgrade for combat operations over Syria – 2016

First Su-33 combat mission – November 16, 2016

First flight J-15D – 2018

SU-33/J-15 VARIANTS

Su-27K – carrier capable Su-27 variant, AL-31F engines

Su-27KUB – side-by-side two-seat prototype, one produced

Su-33 – in-service designation of Su-27K, 24 produced

Su-33D – alternative designation for Su-27KUB

Su-33UB – alternative designation for Su-27KUB

J-15 – Chinese carrierborne fighter combining Su-27 and Su-33 technologies, AL-31 or, later, WS-10B engines, 60 produced to mid-2024

J-15B – projected upgraded operational version employing J-15T technology

J-15D – EW two-seater

J-15S – two-seat J-15

J-15T – prototypes equipped for catapult launch and arrested landings, two produced

A variety of T-10 prototypes and a two-seat Su-27UB performed trials against a take-off ramp on land from August 1982 and by the end of 1987, two Su-27K prototypes had been completed.

On November 1, 1989, a Su-27K landed aboard *Tbilisi*, later renamed *Admiral Kuznetsov*, for the first time. A series of trials followed, including flights by navy pilots from September 1991. The type passed state acceptance trials in 1994. Only 24 from an expected total of 72 was built, plus a single Su-27KUB carrier trainer with side-by-side seating in a new forward fuselage. Various ➤➤

ABOVE: Photographed at Novofedorovka, a Russian military base in Saki, Crimea, in 2010, 'Red 81' has regular Su-33 wing tips. Igor Bubin/ WikimediaCommons

RIGHT: A Su-33 cleans up after taking off from a runway. Dmitry Terekhov/ WikimediaCommons

ABOVE RIGHT: The massive power from two AL-31F3 turbofans launches a Su-33 off *Admiral Kuznetsov's* ski-jump. Vadim Savitsky/ WikimediaCommons

RIGHT: There was a brief period in the 1990s when it seemed the Cold War might never have happened. On February 23 and 24, 1996, *Admiral Kuznetsov* and the Ticonderoga-class cruiser USS *San Jacinto* exercised together in the Mediterranean. US sailors were welcomed aboard the aircraft carrier to view a Su-27K.

levels of upgrade have been applied to the Su-33, although not fleetwide.

Admiral Kuznetsov performed its first deployment in the Mediterranean, with Su-27Ks embarked, between December 1995 and March 1996. The Su-27K was finally accepted for service, as the Su-33, in 1998, but the ship did not sail again until 2000. The Su-33 has been aboard for a handful of subsequent cruises, most recently in 2016, when the ship again sailed into the Mediterranean. This time the aim was to strike targets in Syria and although the Su-33 dropped weapons in anger for the first time, the cruise was marred by the ship's regular breakdowns and the loss of a Su-33 and MiG-29K.

Hopes of selling a Su-33 variant to China for its former Soviet aircraft carrier were dashed by the indigenous J-15, an evolution of the Su-27 design.

Chinese production

Having taken delivery of 78 Flankers from Russian production, in 1997 China began building the aircraft under licence as the Shenyang J-11. With early quality control issues remedied, the aircraft was built in quantity but China became

frustrated with Russia's unwillingness to provide upgraded systems.

The J-11A therefore emerged with some indigenous avionics, before the J-11B appeared, containing sufficient local content for Russia to end the arrangement. The J-11B added air-to-

ground capability to the basic J-11 and provided the basis for the land-based J-11BH naval fighter, while the two-seat J-11BSH is based on the twin-seat J-11BS. The J-11BGH, equipped with AESA radar and based on the upgraded J-11BG emerged sometime around 2019 and it is believed that more recent production aircraft employ the Shenyang WS-10 turbofan.

After Ukraine sold the incomplete Admiral Kuznetsov-class *Varyag* to China following the dissolution of the Soviet Union, the People's Liberation Army Naval Air Force (PLANAF) required a carrierborne fighter to equip the vessel and other aircraft carriers yet to be built. That aircraft was the J-15, combining Su-33 airframe elements with J-11B avionics.

A T-10 prototype of the Su-27K, also supplied by Ukraine, informed the Chinese airframe development, although failed attempts to acquire Su-33s from Russian production

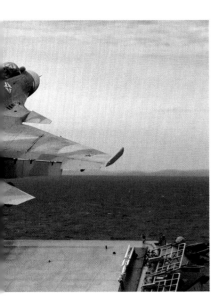

continued until March 2009, just five months before the J-15's first flight on August 31. In May 2010 the J-15 performed its first ski-jump take-offs during land trials, progressing to initial operations from *Liaoning*, the now-finished *Varyag*, in late 2012. J-15 production began in 2013, and the aircraft appears to have performed its first operational cruise in 2017.

As well as installing the WS-10 engine in later J-15 aircraft, Shenyang has produced the two-seat J-15S, the J-15T equipped for catapult launch, the J-15D for electronic warfare and the J-15B, which adds AESA and other advanced systems to the J-15T. The combination of ski-jump launch and arrested landing has limited the heavy J-15's capability off *Liaoning*, however, while technical failures have also caused concern. Design of a next-generation carrierborne fighter is therefore believed under way.

MiG-29K

If the Su-33 is considered an F-14 equivalent in the original timeline of Soviet carrierborne aviation, then the MiG-29K *Fulcrum-D* was comparable to the multi-role F/A-18. Smaller, lighter and offering ground-attack capability lacked by the Su-27K, the MiG-29K was based on the MiG-29M, but considerably altered for carrier use. The wing, intake systems and control surfaces were all re-engineered, while additional fuel tanks, an arrester hook and reinforced undercarriage were added. The first of two MiG-29K prototypes completed its maiden flight on July 23, 1988.

Like the Su-27K, the MiG-29K went to *Tbilisi* for the first time on November 1, 1989. It performed well, but the changing political and military climate led to its cancellation around 1992.

In 2004, the Indian Navy purchased the former Soviet ship *Admiral Gorshkov*, which had operated the V/STOL Yak-38. Modified with a ski-jump and arresting gear, and renamed INS *Vikramaditya*, the vessel's relatively small flight deck area counted against the large Su-33 and the MiG-29K was therefore resurrected.

India ordered an initial 12 MiG-29K single-seat and four MiG-29KUB two-seat jets for delivery from December 2009. In January 2010, it ordered another 29 single-seaters. In February 2010 the MiG became operational on land, INS *Vikramaditya* only becoming available late in 2013.

Early issues with quality control and serviceability appear to have been resolved by late 2018, by which time the Indian Navy had announced its intention to choose between the Super Hornet and Rafale M to equip the forthcoming INS *Vikrant*. A short take-off but arrested landing (STOBAR) carrier like *Vikramaditya*, *Vikrant* received a MiG-29K for the first time on May 26, 2023.

In a peculiar twist of fate, the Russian Navy saw Indian interest in the MiG-29K as an opportunity to order 20 MiG-29KR and four MiG-29KUBR aircraft in 2009, to replace its ageing Su-33s. The purchase was announced in February 2012, ahead of the navy's 2015 decision to upgrade some Su-33s and keep them in service alongside the MiGs.

Four MiGs embarked in *Admiral Kuznetsov* for its ill-fated 2016 Mediterranean combat cruise; one MiG-29KUBR was lost to a crash.

LEFT: A MiG-29KUB performs a touch and go landing on INS *Vikramaditya* in June 2014. Note the folded wings of the similar aircraft spotted on the deck. Indian Navy

LEFT: An Indian Navy MiG-29KUB flies over the deck of USS *Nimitz* during Exercise Malabar 2017, in the Bay of Bengal, on July 16. US Navy

CARRIER COUNTRIES

An increasing number of countries has begun operating aircraft carriers in recent times, with several modifying helicopter carriers for F-35B operations.

Argentina
The veteran ship ARA *Veinticinco de Mayo* kept Argentina in the aircraft carrier business until the late 1980s, when funds for a major refit ran out. Commissioned in 1944 as HMS *Venerable*, the vessel was scrapped from 2000. Its air group latterly comprised the Grumman S-2 Tracker and Douglas A-4 Skyhawk, the Dassault Super Etendard having proven incompatible with it.

Brazil
The Brazilian navy decommissioned BNS *São Paulo* on November 22, 2018, after damage in a second serious onboard fire proved too expensive to repair; the vessel suffered conflagrations in 2005 and 2012. BNS *São Paulo* was a Clemenceau-class carrier originally commissioned by the French navy as *Foch*, on July 15, 1963. Its air wing latterly comprised

the Douglas A-4 Skyhawk and a variety of helicopters.

China
Liaoning, China's first aircraft carrier, was commissioned on September 25, 2012, almost three decades after the vessel had been ordered in 1983 as *Riga*, later *Varyag*, a Kuznetsov-class ship for the Soviet navy. Under construction in Ukraine, it was offered for sale after the USSR's dissolution and passed into Chinese hands between 1998 and 2002.

Refurbished and completed initially as a training carrier, *Liaoning* returned to sea as a Chinese warship in August 2011. One year later it performed trials with J-15 aircraft for the first time.

China's second operational and first indigenously produced carrier, Type 002 ship *Shandong* was commissioned on December 19, 2019. A third ship, the Type 003 *Fujian* began sea trials in May 2024, while a second in the class is being built. A Type 004 vessel is also under construction.

France
FS *Charles de Gaulle* replaced FS *Foch* in French service from

ABOVE: HMS *Kent* **and FS** *Charles De Gaulle* **working together off Djibouti in 2015.** LA(Phot) Simmo Simpson/© UK MoD Crown Copyright 2024

RIGHT: India withdrew the last of its Sea Harriers in 2016. The aircraft latterly operated off INS *Vikramaditya*. Indian Government

BELOW: BNS *São Paulo* (A12), **alongside USS** *Ronald Reagan* **in 2004.** US Navy

2001. Equipped with an air wing comprising Rafale M and the E-2 Hawkeye, plus a variety of helicopters, FS *Charles de Gaulle* has completed several combat deployments, including providing support to the NATO operation over Libya in 2011 and multiple sailings in support of Operation Enduring Freedom over Afghanistan.

Cruises in the Mediterranean and Persian Gulf have launched Rafales on Operation Unified Protector missions, and the carrier exercised in the Mediterranean around the time of Russia's 2022 invasion of Ukraine.

India

Long since a carrier operator, India purchased the former Soviet navy Kiev-class *Admiral Gorshkov* in 2004. Modified extensively in »

work scheduled for completion around 2026. The second vessel, JS *Kaga* was commissioned on March 22, 2017, and began its modification process in 2022. In October 2021, the US Marine Corps operated F-35Bs from JS *Izumo* for the first time.

Russia, it was recommissioned as INS *Vikramaditya* on June 14, 2014.

The ship primarily operates the MiG-29K, but in 2020 hosted the first at-sea trials of the navalised HAL Tejas fighter. Since then, both Indian carriers, INS *Vikramaditya* and INS *Vikrant* have been involved in joint and international exercises.

The Indian Navy decommissioned its previous INS *Vikrant* in 1997. Originally laid down in 1943 as HMS *Hercules*, the ship was commissioned into Indian service in 1961 and latterly operated the Sea Harrier.

Its namesake, the new INS *Vikrant* is the first aircraft carrier built in India. Commissioned on September 2, 2022, it was designed for the MiG-29K, but will operate with an air wing based on the Rafale M and possibly an indigenous future naval fighter.

Italy

ITS *Giuseppe Garibaldi* was built for the Harrier II and commissioned on

September 30, 1985. It first saw combat during Operation Allied Force in 1999 and subsequently during Operation Enduring Freedom in 2001/02 and Operation Unified Protector in 2011.

Since March 27, 2008, ITS *Giuseppe Garibaldi* has served alongside ITS *Cavour*, a new aircraft carrier again designed for the Harrier II. The ship has since been modified to accept the F-35B, entering refit in 2020 and sailing to the US in 2021 for compatibility trials with the Lightning II. Along with ITS *Charles de Gaulle*, ITS *Cavour* was active alongside USS *Harry S Truman* in the Mediterranean around the time of Russia's invasion of Ukraine.

Japan

Japan is modifying both its Izumo-class helicopter-carrying destroyers as light aircraft carriers compatible with the F 35B. Commissioned on March 25, 2015, JS *Izumo* entered conversion in 2020, with further

Russia

Admiral Kuznetsov last deployed operationally in support of Russian forces in Syria during 2016/17, flying its MiG-29KR and Su-33 fighters on combat missions. Plagued by unreliability and mishap, the vessel is expected to be retired in 2025 and is unlikely to return to sea.

Spain

Another 'Harrier carrier', Spain's ESPS *Príncipe de Asturias* was commissioned on May 30, 1988, and decommissioned in 2013. The Spanish navy now sends its Harriers to see in ESPS *Juan Carlos I*, a ship commissioned in September 2010 as a landing helicopter dock.

Thailand

Commissioned as a light aircraft carrier in 1997, Thailand's HTMS *Chakri Naruebet* was built to operate first-generation Harriers in the form of AV-8S Matador aircraft bought second hand from Spain. By 2006 it had become impossible to support the Matadors and they were removed from service. An attempt to purchase ex-Royal Navy Sea Harrier FA.Mk 2 aircraft

had already failed, leaving the Royal Thai Navy with no choice but to operate the ship only with helicopters and in a variety of humanitarian relief operations. It seems unlikely that HTMS *Chakri Naruebet* remains in regular use.

Turkey

Based on the Juan Carlos-class design, Turkey's TCG *Anadolu* was designed as a helicopter carrier but modified in-build for the F-35B. After Turkey committed to buying the S-400 air defence system from Russia, however, it was removed from the F-35 programme in 2019. The ship therefore entered service as a helicopter and potential UAV carrier. A second vessel, TCG *Trakya*, may also be built.

LEFT: This Spanish AV-8B Harrier II Plus had flown off ESPS *Juan Carlos I* onto USS *Wasp* in the Baltic Sea on June 15, 2024, during the Baltic Operations 2024 exercise. US Navy

BOTTOM: TCG *Anadolu* in the Mediterranean in August 2023. US Navy

BELOW: HTMS *Chakri Naruebet* in the South China Sea during 2003 with a Matador on deck. US Navy

ODYSSEY DAWN, HARMATTAN, ELLAMY AND UNIFIED PROTECTOR

Conducted in 2011 to enforce United Nations Security Council Resolutions 1970 and 1973, Operation Unified Protector employed French and Italian aircraft carriers.

ABOVE: Landing back aboard USS *Kearsarge* in the Mediterranean on March 21, 2011, this US Marine Corps Harrier was returning from an Odyssey Dawn air strike.
US Marine Corps

Discontent in several Arab countries found new voice through social media, first resulting in social unrest in Tunisia in December 2010 that overthrew the government in January 2011. Similar protests followed in Algeria later in December, spreading in 2011 to other countries, including Egypt, Iraq, Bahrain and Libya. Unrest broke out in Libya on February 15 and quickly escalated into an uprising against Muammar Gaddafi's government.

Forces opposing Gaddafi created a National Transitional Council and this entered into open conflict with troops loyal to the government. They used brutal tactics against National Transitional Council rebels, protesters and the population at large, attacking medical workers treating injured civilians for example. Anyone, civilian, militia or otherwise, judged to be anti-government became a target.

In response, United Nations Security Council Resolutions (UNSCR) 1970 and 1973 were issued, imposing sanctions and proposing a no-fly zone. Importantly, NATO was authorised to use any means necessary to protect the civilian population, short of placing troops on the ground. Individual NATO members began launching their own operations while a full NATO response was formulated, the UK's Operation Ellamy, France's Operation Harmattan and, for the US, Operation Odyssey Dawn, most significant among them. On March 31, 2011, NATO took full responsibility for enforcing the UN resolutions under Operation Unified Protector.

Shipborne aviation

Ships in the Mediterranean took an important role in the campaign, firing missiles, employing naval gunfire and launching aircraft. US carrier aircraft were not involved, but France, Italy and the UK all made extensive use of shipborne assets.

France deployed Gazelle, Tiger and Puma helicopters in the landing helicopter dock vessel *Tonnerre*, and Rafale M, Super Etendard and Hawkeye fixed-wing aircraft from *Charles de Gaulle*, which also embarked its regular helicopter detachment and two air force Caracal helicopters. The Italian navy employed *Giuseppe Garibaldi*, equipped with Harriers and Merlin helicopters.

and *Giuseppe Garibaldi* began operations over Libya on March 24, 2011, its eight Harriers operating similarly to the French Rafales and other fast jet assets in theatre. The UK flew fixed-wing combat aircraft from bases in the UK and Italy during Operation Ellamy, adding Apache capability from May 27, when HMS *Ocean* arrived off Libya.

Its gunship complement swelled from three to five helicopters as the mission progressed.

The conflict ended after October 20, when NATO apparently unknowingly attacked a convoy in which Gaddafi was riding. He was captured and killed by rebel troops. Operation Unified Protector closed on October 31, 2011.

ABOVE: Denied the capability of its recently retired carriers, the UK flew Army Air Corps Apache helicopters off HMS *Ocean* during Operation Ellamy. This photograph was taken over the Mediterranean Sea on July 11, 2011. LA(Phot) Guy Pool/© UK MoD Crown Copyright 2024

Having relinquished its carriers and Harriers in 2010, the UK later deployed HMS *Ocean*, a landing platform helicopter ship with Army Air Corps Apache attack helicopters embarked. The US deployed amphibious assault ships equipped with Harriers and helicopters, plus several other helicopter-capable vessels, but chose to keep its long-term involvement low key.

Charles de Gaulle took up station off Libya on March 22, 2011, its F3 standard Rafale Ms initially flying reconnaissance missions. Similar sorties continued on the 23rd, alongside the Super Etendard, and on the 24th, the Aéronavale expended ordnance over Libya for the first time. On the 27th, *Charles de Gaulle's* Rafales joined air force Rafales flying from France in a joint attack on a command centre, setting the tone for continued operations even as Harmattan merged into Unified Protector, fully under NATO command, on March 31.

Operation Unified Protector had begun on March 23, 2011,

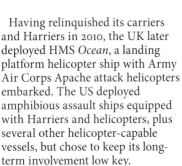

LEFT: *Charles de Gaulle* embarked two AS365F Dauphin helicopters for plane guard and rescue duties. This example visited USS *Mount Whitney* on March 21, 2011. US Navy

LEFT: An HSC-22 MH-60S refuels aboard the amphibious transport dock ship USS *Ponce*. With four Hellfires to port and door machine guns, the aircraft was heavily armed for an Odyssey Dawn mission on March 25, 2011. Specialist aviation fuel personnel on US Navy ships wear purple shirts and are affectionately known as 'grapes'. US Navy

DASSAULT RAFALE M

The superlative Dassault Rafale successfully satisfies the requirements of shore and ship as the fully navalised Rafale M.

RIGHT: A Rafale M takes fuel from a US Air Force KC-135 tanker on an April 10, 2021, Operation Inherent Resolve mission. The aircraft has an Armement Air-Sol Modulaire (AASM) Hammer precision-guided missile under a rack on its outer wing pylon and MICA AAMs at its wing tips. The large underwing stores are fuel tanks, while a TALIOS targeting pod is mounted under the fuselage.
US Air Force

The Rafale M's roots reach back to the mid-1970s, when France, Germany and the UK launched the European Combat Aircraft (ECA) study, although the three nations' requirements quickly diverged. Nonetheless, in 1983 a new project was established. Known as the European Fighter Aircraft (EFA), it was a five-nation programme since Italy and Spain had joined the ECA countries.

France believed EFA would not produce a good match for its operational requirements and was unhappy with the allocation of design leadership. It therefore began work on its own Avion de Combat Experimentale (ACX). In 1983, the UK flew an Experimental Aircraft Programme (EAP) demonstrator for the EFA, a machine remarkably like the Eurofighter Typhoon that eventually matured from the EFA concept.

In August 1985, France withdrew from EFA in favour of its own Avion de Combat Tactique (ACT) programme, well placed to begin demonstrator flying with the Dassault ACX. If the EAP looked a lot like Typhoon, then ACX looked even more like Rafale, to the extent that it was named Rafale A during its test campaign. It flew for the first time on July 4, 1986, and completed 460 trial flights, including touch-and-go landings aboard the French aircraft carrier *Clemenceau*, before an M88 turbofan replaced one of its F404 engines for continued test work. The M88 was intended for the production Rafale.

By the time of the Rafale A's 865th and final flight on January 24, 1994, the Rafale C prototype had already been flying almost three years. The standard single-seat configuration for the French air force and export, Rafale C flew for the first time on May 19, 1991, followed by the two-seat Rafale B prototype on April 30, 1993. The most pressing French requirement, however, was replacement of the Aéronavale's Vought F-8 Crusader. In 1989, consideration had been given to buying the F/A-18 Hornet, but instead the Avion Combat Marine, later Rafale Marine, or Rafale M was developed.

The first of two Rafale M prototypes completed its maiden flight on December 12, 1991, embodying significant changes compared to the land-based Rafale C. The undercarriage was strengthened, and the nose gear fitted with a so-called 'jump strut' and catapult towbar. The former pushes the aircraft's nose up at launch, while the latter engages the catapult shuttle. Previous French carrierborne aircraft had employed launch strops and the towbar was therefore a new innovation for the country.

The first prototype was tested extensively on land in the US before going to the ship, the Clemenceau-class vessel *Foch*, for the first time on April 1, 1993. Meanwhile, the post-Cold War 'peace dividend' that affected contemporaneous US naval aircraft programmes including the A-12, caused a reduction in funding and consequent slowing »

RIGHT: The carrier strike groups of USS *George HW Bush, Charles de Gaulle* and the Italian navy's *Cavour* gathered in the Ionian Sea for multi-carrier operations in November 2022. There was no doubting the provenance of this Rafale M as it performed a touch-and-go on the US carrier.
US Navy

RIGHT: Exercise Neptune Shield 22 saw NATO assets, including this F3 standard Rafale M (lead) and VFA-211 F/A-18E, working together over the Mediterranean.
US Navy

LEFT: Rafale presents an unusual shape, with its 'pinched' lower forward fuselage, large intakes, canards and prominent canopy. This 17F Rafale M was visiting USS *George HW Bush* in the Atlantic in May 2018. US Navy

RAFALE M DATA	
Length	15.30m (50ft 2.5in)
Wingspan	10.90m (35ft 8in)
Height	5.30m (17ft 5in)
Empty weight class	10,000kg (22,000lb)
Maximum take-off weight	24,500kg (54,000lb)
Maximum weapon load	9,500kg (21,000lb)
Maximum speed	Mach 1.8
Climb rate	305m/s (60,000ft/min)
Combat range, three tanks, two SCALP-EG, two MICA	1,850km (1,150 miles)
Engines	Two SAFRAN M88-4E turbofans each rated at 75kN (17,000lb) with afterburner
Armament	One internal 30mm GIAT 30/M791 cannon; MICA EM, MICA IR and Meteor AAMs; air-to-ground stores include Apache, SCALP-EG, AASM Hammer, AM39 Exocet, Paveway-series LGBs and ASMP-A
Orders (all versions, production continuing)	**234 (France), 261 (Export)**

RAFALE TIMELINE
First flight Rafale A demonstrator – July 4, 1986
First flight Rafale C – May 19, 1991
First flight Rafale M – December 12, 1991
First Rafale M at-sea trials – April 1993
First flight Rafale B – April 30, 1993
First flight production Rafale B – November 24, 1998
First flight production Rafale M – July 7, 1999
First Rafale M delivery – December 2000
Rafale M Mission Héraclès/Operation Enduring Freedom – 2002
Rafale M F1 operational – June 2004
First Rafale M F2 delivery – May 2006
First F3 standard Rafale delivered – 2008
Cross-deck exercise with USS *Harry S Truman* – June 4, 2010
Opération Harmattan – March 19 – March 31, 2011
Operation Unified Protector – March 23 – October 31, 2011
Rafale M Operation Inherent Resolve – 2016
First F4 standard Rafale delivered – 2023
India announced intention to purchase 26 Rafale M – July 14, 2023
First Standard F4 Rafale C operational – February 16, 2024

FRENCH RAFALE VARIANTS
Rafale A – Avion de Combat Experimental (ACX) demonstrator, F404 engines, 1 produced
Rafale B – two-seater for French Air and Space Force and export, M88 engines, in production
Rafale C – single-seater for French Air and Space Force, M88 engines, in production
Rafale M – single-seater for French Navy, M88 engines, in production
Standard F1 – initial production standard, air-to-air only
Standard F2 – air-to-air and initial air-to-ground standard
Standard F3 – expanded capability, including ASMP-A and reconnaissance pod compatibility, new build aircraft and upgrades
Standard F4 – further upgrade, especially to connectivity
Standard F5 – expected upgrade standard from mid-2030s

in Rafale development. The first production Rafale B therefore only took its first flight on November 24, 1998, the first production Rafale M following it into the air on July 7, 1999; all Rafale pilots train on the B-model, so although it is nominally an air force asset it has great significance to the navy training 'pipeline'.

Given the urgent priority for replacing its Crusaders, the Aéronavale was first to take production Rafales, in December 2000. The Rafale M went to sea in the new carrier *Charles de Gaulle* in 2001 but was only deemed fully operational in 2004. The aircraft is compatible with US Navy carrier

25

USS *Dwight D Eisenhower* receives a flyby from a tight formation of Rafale Ms. The French and US assets were deployed for Operation Inherent Resolve, in December 2016. US Navy

decks and in June 2010 a cross-decking exercise with USS *Harry S Truman* saw French pilots qualify against the ship.

Upgrades to weapons and systems continue to expand Rafale capability, particularly through a series of 'F' standards. Early Rafale Ms were delivered to F1 standard, equipped only for air-to-air work. In 2006, F2 arrived, with air-to-ground capability, and from 2008, F3 standard aircraft have been compatible with the nuclear Air-Sol Moyenne Portée-Amélioré (ASMP-A, improved medium-range air-to-surface missile). The latest F4 standard became operational in 2024.

LEFT: Here projecting ahead of the nose undercarriage, the towbar engages in the catapult shuttle and is a key Rafale M feature. This was a July 2018 touch down on USS *Harry S Truman.* US Navy

CARRIER CONVOLUTIONS

The convoluted post-Falklands War story of the UK's aircraft capability is one of short-sighted decision making and ill-considered cost cutting.

I n the years following the 1982 Falklands War, the Royal Navy consolidated its airpower around three Invincible-class carriers. The conflict was fought with the first of these, HMS *Invincible*, sailing alongside the much older HMS *Hermes*, a vessel sold to India in 1986 for continued service as INS *Viraat* until its withdrawal in 2017.

Meanwhile, the Invincible-class was completed with HMS *Illustrious* and HMS *Ark Royal*, each of them typically embarking an air wing based on the Sea Harrier and Sea King AEW (airborne early warning), the latter introduced as a rapidly developed capability after the Falklands War demonstrated a gap in the Royal Navy's radar coverage.

In 1993, the upgraded Sea Harrier FA.Mk 2 entered service, its Blue Vixen radar and AIM-120 missile armament arguably placing it among the most capable air-to-air platforms of the day. HMS *Invincible* took the Sea Harrier FA2 into combat over Bosnia in 1994. Later the ship supported Operation Southern Watch, before returning

BELOW: This Sea Harrier FA.Mk 2 was aboard HMS *Illustrious* in the Persian Gulf in 1998. US Navy

to the Balkans for Operation Allied Force.

The FA2 represented the ultimate iteration of the first-generation Harrier, while the Royal Air Force had begun operating the Harrier II, most significantly with the introduction of the Harrier GR.Mk 7 in 1990. In 2000, *Invincible* was modified for compatibility with the RAF Harrier but then effectively mothballed in August 2005. Under

the UK's notorious 2010 Strategic Defence and Security Review (SDSR), the Harrier was removed from service and *Invincible* sold for scrap.

HMS *Illustrious* was hurriedly completed to relieve *Invincible* in the South Atlantic. Later, it served on Operation Deny Flight and Operation Southern Watch, and Operation Palliser, a successful British intervention in Sierra Leone's 2000

civil war. After conflict broke out in Lebanon in 2006, *Illustrious* helped evacuate British citizens trapped by the fighting. It was lucky to escape the 2010 SDSR, albeit without Harriers. HMS *Illustrious* continued in service as a helicopter carrier until 2014, when it was decommissioned.

HMS *Ark Royal* was commissioned on November 1, 1985. It too saw service off the Balkans, before supporting Operation Iraqi　》

RIGHT: HMS *Illustrious* prepares to receive a Sea Harrier FA2, with an AEW-configured Sea King already on deck. The ship was off the North Carolina coast in 1998. Royal Navy/ © UK MoD Crown Copyright 2024

BELOW: The Harrier II brought enhanced ground-attack capability to Royal Navy carriers, but significant air-to-air capability was lost in 2006 when the Sea Harrier was retired. Here two Harriers, the lead aircraft a GR.Mk 7A, are coming aboard HMS *Illustrious* during Exercise Joint Warrior 2008. LA(Phot) Des Wade/© UK MoD Crown Copyright 2024

Freedom, although with only helicopters embarked. The 2010 SDSR consigned *Ark Royal* to scrap and it was decommissioned in 2011.

Queen Elizabeth Class

Ordered in 2008, the Queen Elizabeth Class comprises two aircraft carriers optimised for the F-35B, known in UK service as Lightning, not Lightning II. HMS *Queen Elizabeth* was commissioned on December 7, 2017, and HMS *Prince of Wales* on December 10, 2019. The carriers survived the 2010 SDSR, although the government considered changing the design to CATOBAR from STOVL to support the longer-ranged, more capable F-35C, but the cost of redesign proved prohibitive. The vessels emerged with distinctive twin island superstructures and equipped for an air group comprising F-35B jets, and Merlin and Wildcat helicopters.

Considerably larger than the Invincible-class ships, the Queen Elizabeth Class is the centrepiece of the UK Carrier Strike Group. After a series of sea trials had proven the ship and its ability to safely operate the F-35B and a variety of UK and other helicopters, in May 2021 HMS *Queen Elizabeth* departed as the lead ship of Carrier Strike Group 21.

The ship embarked a mixed force of UK and US Marine Corps F-35Bs, taking them as far as the South China Sea. On the way, the vessel undertook its and the UK F-35's first combat operations, launching Operation Inherent Resolve missions.

On the return leg the carrier lost an F-35B into the Mediterranean, the pilot ejecting successfully.

In 2023, HMS *Queen Elizabeth* embarked upon a cruise designed to show its interoperability with other European navies and send a message to Russia.

SDSR 2010 stated the UK's requirement at one aircraft carrier, and it seemed for a while that HMS *Prince of Wales* might be delivered into storage. In the event, it was delivered as a fully functioning ship and will complete its first operational cruise, to the Pacific, in 2025.

Finally, it is worth noting that the UK's second frontline F-35B squadron, 809 Naval Air Squadron was re-established in December 2023 and flew its first mission from the Lightning's base at RAF Marham, Norfolk, on July 15, 2024.

NORTHROP GRUMMAN E-2 HAWKEYE

Few military aircraft have seen the transformation in capability enjoyed by the E-2. First flown in the early 1960s, it will remain a key command and control asset into the 2040s.

RIGHT: This VAW-116 E-2C was recovering from a Southern Seas 2024 mission aboard USS *George Washington* in the Atlantic Ocean. The distinctive intake aft of the cockpit contains a radiator for cooling the aircraft's avionics.

All US Navy

Among the most visually distinctive aircraft ever built, the Grumman (later Northrop Grumman) E-2 Hawkeye has proven remarkably adaptable to technological advance, such that it is among today's most effective airborne command and control and battlespace management platforms yet looks little different externally to the prototype W2F-1 that flew for the first time on October 21, 1960.

That the Hawkeye airframe is old enough to have appeared prior to the 1962 reconciliation of US military designation systems to the now familiar 'role designator-model number' format says much for the quality of Grumman's original design. The initial prototype was aerodynamically representative of the production configuration, with a 24ft (7.32m) diameter rotodome for the antenna of its AN/APS-111 radar and a distinctive tail unit, mounting four fins and sharply dihedralled tailplanes. The latter was found necessary to counter the complex airflow around the rotodome.

BELOW: Riding the lift to USS *Theodore Roosevelt's* flightdeck, this pair of E-2C Hawkeyes demonstrates the eight-bladed NP2000 propeller to advantage.

A mission-equipped W2F-1 flew for the first time on April 29, 1961, and deliveries of the E-2A Hawkeye began on January 19, 1964. The aircraft was therefore available for combat during the protracted war in Vietnam, albeit somewhat unreliably given the propensity for mission suite failures. The technical nature of its mission meant the E-2 was always going to be challenging and subject to upgrade. The first of many improvement packages added a Litton microcomputer and other

avionics changes, addressing some of the early unreliability. An E-2A so modified flew for the first time in February 1969 and a further 49 E-2As were upgraded to a similar E-2B standard.

E-2C

Far more ambitious in scope, a modified E-2A flew as the E-2C prototype for the first time on January 20, 1971. Revised mission avionics included AN/APS-120 radar, a new computer and other supporting

equipment; there was also more power, from uprated T56 engines.

After a second converted E-2A joined the programme, the E-2C was ready for service from November 1973. The E-2C remained as the only Hawkeye variant flying off US Navy carrier decks until 2014, when the E-2D achieved IOC. The simple designation is misleading however, since the later E-2C standard is quite different to that of 40 years earlier.

From the 34th production E-2C, AN/APS-125 radar replaced AN/APS-120, the former being retrofitted to in-service aircraft too. Another engine upgrade saw the T56-A-425 replace the -422; this aircraft configuration was later labelled E-2C Group 0.

Delivered from 1989, updated E-2C Group I aircraft replaced AN/APS-125 with AN/APS-138, later -139, and enjoyed improved processing and motive capability, the latter via -427 engines. Group II production began in the early 1990s, further upgrading the radar to AN/APS-145 standard and adding new mission systems that reflected the increasingly data-driven nature of warfare, the Joint Tactical Information Distribution System (JTIDS) data link and GPS among them.

Further upgrades to cockpit and mission avionics occurred, before the final E-2C mission system upgrade came with the Hawkeye 2000 standard. The mission computer was upgraded, and the aircraft made compatible with the US Navy's Cooperative Engagement Capability

(CEC) data link. Since its earliest days, the Hawkeye had been intended as an integrated component within a network of ship and aircraft sensor systems and with Hawkeye 2000 that objective was achieved within the concept of Aegis, making the Hawkeye 2000 part of the Theater Air Missile Defense (TAMD) system.

Several air arms purchased Hawkeyes as a cost-effective alternative to the E-3 AWACS. Among them, only France has taken the aircraft to sea, in *Charles de Gaulle*. Three E-2Cs were delivered from 1998, Flottille 4F becoming operational with the aircraft in 2000.

From 2007, the Hawkeye 2000 was further upgraded to improve processing speed and add satellite communications among other mission capabilities, while the

cockpits of many aircraft became fully glass. These changes came on top of a universal change to the eight-bladed NP2000 propeller from 2004. More efficient, the NP2000 is also easier to maintain and reduces vibration.

Advanced Hawkeye

Visually significant, the NP2000 is carried over onto the E-2D Advanced Hawkeye, the latest E-2 variant and one which again deviates remarkably little from the W2F-1 externally. First flown on August 3, 2007, the E-2D has a new AN/APY-9 AESA radar system, bucking the trend established by previous Hawkeye upgrades where each radar has been an iterative improvement of the last. Its computers, radios, satellite **»**

LEFT: The Hawkeye's wide wingspan means it demands respect during operations off the carrier. This VAW-115 E-2C was preparing to launch off USS *Theodore Roosevelt* in the Pacific during May 2021.

BOTTOM LEFT: The E-2A and E-2B featured a shorter, blunt nose profile. This E-2B was aboard USS *Coral Sea*, a Midway-class carrier decommissioned in 1990. These ships were smaller than the Nimitz class, making Hawkeye operations even more demanding.

BOTTOM RIGHT: Group II E-2Cs feature new equipment installations under the centre fuselage and in the centre of the main antenna radome. This aircraft was departing USS *Nimitz* for a June 2023 mission over the Pacific.

Greyhound

Grumman's S2F-1 Tracker ASW aircraft entered US Navy service in February 1954. The versatile airframe was subsequently modified as the TF-1 (later C-1) Trader, a carrier onboard delivery (COD) aircraft designed to move freight, mail and passengers between aircraft carriers and shore bases. The Trader airframe was then heavily modified as the WF-2 (later E-1) Tracer airborne early warning aircraft, mounting a large radome above its fuselage. After the US Navy chose the Hawkeye to replace the E-1, Grumman was quick to offer an E-2 derivative equivalent to the C-1.

The C-2 Greyhound combined the wings, empennage and engines of the E-2A with a new fuselage offering a tail ramp and space for up to 39 passengers. Two E-2As provided components towards a pair of YC-2A prototypes, the first making its maiden flight on November 18, 1964. Delivery of 17 aircraft began in 1965, for service entry from 1966.

In 1984, a further 39 aircraft were procured as replacements for the older machines and fleet expansion. Retaining the C-2A designation, they were nonetheless equipped with improved airframe and avionics components. A subsequent service life extension programme (SLEP) installed NP2000 propellers, navigation improvements in common with the upgraded E-2C Group II standard, and lengthened airframe life.

In 2015, the US Navy signed a memorandum of understanding (MoU) for the HV-22B tiltrotor, based on the MV-22B Osprey and optimised for the COD role. It ordered 48 redesignated CMV-22B aircraft in 2018, although this number was later reduced to 44. First flight came in December 2019 and IOC on December 14, 2021.

The CMV-22B completed its first West Coast operational deployment on February 17, 2022, and is expected to take over East Coast COD duties in 2025, when the last C-2A is likely to be withdrawn.

ABOVE: The Greyhound's rear ramp/door is obvious as this aircraft leaves USS *Ronald Reagan* in the Philippine Sea during June 2022.

ABOVE: The C-2A squadrons maintained detachments globally to support US Navy carriers wherever in the world they deployed. This aircraft was with Detachment 5 of VRC-30 in 2022.

HAWKEYE DATA	
E-2D	
Length	17.60m (57ft 8.75in)
Wingspan	24.56m (80ft 7in)
Height	5.58m (18ft 3.75in)
Empty weight	19,536kg (43,068lb)
Maximum gross weight	26,083kg (57,500lb)
Maximum speed	648km/h (350mph)
Endurance with air-to-air refuelling	12 hours
Engines	Two Rolls-Royce T56-A-427A turboprops each rated at 3,751kW (5,100eshp)
All variants (production continues), more than	**300**

HAWKEYE TIMELINE
First flight W2F-1 – October 21, 1960
First flight W2F-1 with mission avionics – April 29, 1961
Redesignation to E-2 – 1962
First E-2A delivery – January 19, 1964
First E-2A combat cruise to Southeast Asia – 1965
First flight of E-2B upgrade of E-2A – 1969
First flight E-2C prototype – January 20, 1971
E-2C service entry – November 1973
First E-2C operational deployment – 1974
E-2C Group 0 service entry – 1980
Operation El Dorado Canyon – April 15, 1986
E-2C Group I service entry – August 1989
Operation Desert Shield – 1990-91
Operation Desert Storm – 1991
Operation Southern Watch – 1992-2003
E-2C Group II service entry – June 1992
Operation Deny Flight – 1993-95
Operation Northern Watch – 1997-2003
First E-2C delivery to France – 1998
Operation Desert Fox – 1998
Operation Allied Force – 1999
French E-2C becomes operational – 2000
Operation Enduring Freedom – 2001-14
Operation Iraqi Freedom – 2003-10
Upgrade to NP2000 propeller began – 2004
First flight E-2D – August 3, 2007
First E-2D operational delivery – 2010
Operation New Dawn – 2010-11
E-2D IOC – 2014
Operation Inherent Resolve – 2014-present
First operational US Navy E-2D squadron inflight refuelling qualified – 2020
French commitment to purchase three E-2D – 2021
Operation Prosperity Guardian – 2023-present

US NAVY HAWKEYE VARIANTS

W2F-1 – aerodynamic first prototype and mission-equipped prototype, Allison T56 engines, 2 produced

E-2A – first production standard, Allison T56 engines, APS-96 radar, 59 produced

TE-2A – crew training aircraft, 4 produced

E-2B – upgrade of E-2A, digital mission computer, 50 produced

E-2C prototype – two conversions from E-2A

E-2C Group 0 – retrospective designation for initial E-2C model, T56-A-425 engines, APS-120 (APS-125 from 1976) radar

E-2C Group I – T56-A-427 engines, APS-138 radar

E-2C Group II – APS-145 radar

E-2C Group II Plus/Hawkeye 2000 – upgrade of E-2C Group II

TE-2C – crew training aircraft, 4 produced

E-2D Advanced Hawkeye – New cockpit and avionics, Rolls-Royce T56-A-427A engines, AN/APY-9 radar

communications and cockpit are all new, the latter enabling the co-pilot to reconfigure his or her displays to enable support to the mission crew.

Cooperative Engagement Capability is a key E-2D function within the Naval Integrated Fire Control – Counter Air (NIFC-CA) concept, which employs the SM-6 interceptor missile as its primary kill vehicle. US Navy destroyers began fielding SM-6 launch batteries as long ago as 2017, but the E-2D now provides a significant and proven over-the-horizon targeting capability against anti-ship missiles. Interestingly, an F-35 or suitably equipped drone could also stand in for the E-2D, although without its persistence or the benefit of human operators and extensive sensor suite, respectively. France committed to a three-aircraft purchase to replace its E-2C fleet in 2021, with deliveries expected to be complete by 2028.

Planned from the outset, inflight refuelling is another important E-2D capability. The US Navy declared IOC with the aircraft in 2014, but only in 2020 did the first operational E-2D squadron complete its air-to-air refuelling training. While E-2D production continues, it is worth noting that those aircraft equipped with inflight refuelling probes also feature 'high endurance' crew seats, an enhanced fuel system and new exterior lighting. The E-2D is likely to become the baseline for future Hawkeye variants and there is every indication that the type will remain in service into the 2040s.

LEFT: Inflight refuelling greatly increases the E-2D's time on station. The inflight refuelling probe installation is practical rather than elegant.

LEFT: Proving the E-2D's air-to-air refuelling capability has involved compatibility tests against various tankers, including the US Air Force KC-46A Pegasus. On this April 16, 2024, sortie, a VX-20 E-2D, up from Naval Air Station Patuxent River, Maryland, worked with a 412th Test Wing Pegasus.

GERALD R FORD CLASS

The Gerald R Ford-class aircraft carriers are likely to keep delivering US Navy airpower to 2100 and beyond.

On May 3, 1975, the US Navy commissioned USS *Nimitz*, the first of ten Nimitz-class ships, the last of which, USS *George HW Bush*, was commissioned on January 10, 2009. The new ships gradually replaced carriers of previous classes, leaving USS *Enterprise* and USS *John F Kennedy* as the only non-Nimitz vessels remaining in service until March 23, 2007, when *JFK* was decommissioned, and February 3, 2017, when *Enterprise* left the fleet.

The Gerald R Ford-class (or simply Ford-class) was procured in 2008 to replace USS *Enterprise* and USS *John F Kennedy* and, presumably, the Nimitz-class as they reach or exceed their expected 50-year service life. To date, the US Navy has announced plans for four new ships, USS *Gerald R Ford*, USS *John F Kennedy*, USS *Enterprise* and USS *Doris Miller*, but more are likely.

Commissioned on July 22, 2017, the lead ship emerged from 18 months of Post Delivery Test & Trials (PDT&T) and Combat Systems

Ship's Qualification Trials (CSSQT) in August 2021 and entered service in 2022. The second ship, USS *John F Kennedy* is expected to be commissioned in 2025.

New features

Although its hull design is similar to that of the Nimitz-class, the Ford-class is recognisable by the aft location of its island. Its deck lifts are also re-engineered and relocated for more efficient flight deck operations. The more fundamental changes are internal, however and primarily affect two evolving aspects of naval warfare: the burgeoning requirement for electrical power and changing crew composition.

The Nimitz-class is close to reaching the extent of its electrical capacity, modern weapon systems and other modifications having drawn upon the generating capacity of the two A4W reactors installed in each ship. Smaller, more powerful A1B reactors equip the Ford-class, requiring a reduced

crew to manage yet generating at least 25% more power than the A4W. The fraction of that power allocated to electricity generation is increased by 300%, reflecting the systems already installed in the ship and the requirements of future upgrades, including the potential addition of directed energy weapons.

Among the significant electrical systems in the Ford-class, an Electromagnetic Aircraft Launch System (EMALS) replaces the traditional steam catapult. The latter requires a supply of desalinated water – created from sea water in an energy intensive process – to drive a steam piston that accelerates an aircraft along the deck. Rather than a piston, EMALS employs a linear induction motor for a smoother acceleration that creates less stress on airframes and may be applied to lighter and heavier aircraft than those compatible with steam catapults.

Advanced Arresting Gear stops aircraft on landing, using

BELOW: Ships from the Gerald R Ford Carrier Strike Group and Bataan Amphibious Ready Group, plus the Hellenic navy frigate HS *Navarinon* sail in formation in the Mediterranean Sea on December 31, 2023. USS *Gerald R Ford* is leading the Wasp-class amphibious assault ship USS *Bataan*, demonstrating the difference in size and configuration between what are effectively two different aircraft carrier designs.

All US Navy

RIGHT: Sailing alongside one another in the Atlantic Ocean on June 4, 2020, the aft position of USS *Gerald R Ford's* (CVN 78) island superstructure compared to that of the Nimitz-class aircraft carrier USS *Harry S Truman* (CVN 75) is obvious.

BELOW: USS *Gerald R Ford* transited the Strait of Gibraltar on January 5, 2023, its presence in the region sending a clear message to friend and potential foe alike.

electrically-driven systems to create smoother deceleration and suiting the carrier to lighter aircraft. The ship's dual-band radar is another major electricity consumer, while much of its defensive weapons system also relies on electrical power.

Greater use of automation and better design enables the Ford-class to sail with a crew reduced by as much as 700 sailors across the ship and air wing staff. Its accommodation has been designed with gender neutral heads and related facilities, reflecting the shift in gender ratio aboard ship; it is likely that an even larger proportion of a future Ford-class's 2,600 or so crew will be female and the ships are designed for this and other future upgrades.

The Ford-class and Nimitz-class vessels are 332.85m (1,092ft long) and have a beam of 40.84m (134ft). The Nimitz-class flight deck is 76.80m (252ft) wide and that of the Ford-class 78.03m (256ft). At full load, both classes displace around 100,000 tons and both ship types can exceed 30kt (56km/h).

LOCKHEED MARTIN F-35 LIGHTNING II

Although the Lightning II is still a long way from operational maturity, its F-35B and F-35C models are already revolutionising naval airpower.

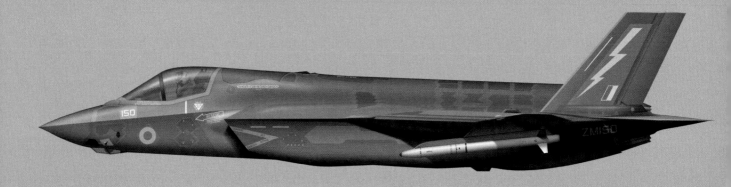

BELOW: The UK operates a joint Lightning Force, staffed by Royal Air Force and Royal Navy personnel. On March 5, 2024, HMS *Prince of Wales* deployed for the Arctic Circle, where it operated its F-35B jets in Exercise Nordic Response 24. AS1 Amber Mayall/© UK MoD Crown Copyright 2024

ew aviation stories are longer, more complicated and, with an eye to the future, ultimately perhaps as successful, as that of Lockheed Martin's F-35. It begins in 1983, when the US Navy launched its Advanced Tactical Aircraft (ATA) programme. Elsewhere, an ambitious requirement for a supersonic Harrier replacement saw the Defense Advanced Research Projects Agency (DARPA) instigate the Advanced Short Take-Off/Vertical Landing (ASTOVL) project: 1983 was a busy year for futuristic aircraft concepts and acronyms.

Intended to create a stealthy replacement for the A-6 Intruder, ATA produced the McDonnell Douglas/General Dynamics A-12 design. Always destined to be technically challenging, the A-12 was also costly, and ATA was abandoned in 1991 as the effects of the post-Cold War 'peace dividend' took hold.

With future requirements to replace the Harriers in USMC and Royal Air Force service, and Royal Navy Sea Harriers, the US and UK were hoping key data would emerge from ASTOVL, which comprised two classified programmes. Running from 1987 to 1994, the STOVL Strike Fighter (SSF) programme considered stealthy, supersonic STOVL fighter technologies, while the year-long Common Affordable Lightweight Fighter (CALF) effort began in 1993 and fed ASTOVL and SSF data into a US/UK Harrier replacement document.

Meanwhile, the US Navy had also been examining possibilities for a fleet defender to replace the F-14 Tomcat. Active since the early 1980s, in 1990 the US Air Force's Advanced Tactical Fighter (ATF) campaign produced flying demonstrators of the Lockheed YF-22 and Northrop YF-23. In April 1991, the YF-22 was selected, leading to the Lockheed Martin F-22 Raptor. The basic design might also have produced the F-14 replacement, under the Naval ATF (NATF) concept, but was soon abandoned as too expensive.

More programmes

While ATF was flying demonstrators, the USAF turned to the F-16, for which it planned to find a successor under the Multi-Role Fighter (MRF) programme. By 1992, MRF was also looking to replace Fairchild Republic A-10A Thunderbolt II attack aircraft

ABOVE: This June 21, 2022, F-35C test flight out of NAS Patuxent River, Maryland shows the aircraft equipped with underwing pylons carrying JDAM bombs and AIM-9X AAMs. Working with the Pax River F-35 Integrated Test Force, VX-23 trials weapons and systems before they go to the front line. First flown in May 2011, F-35C CF-03 has long been part of the VX-23 fleet.
US Navy

LEFT: The X-35B demonstrates its hover configuration over Edward AFB, California on July 11, 2001.
Lockheed Martin

and the US Navy Hornet fleet. But the scarce funding of the immediate post-Cold War period saw the USAF abandon MRF in favour of upgrading its F-16s and, ultimately A-10s; MRF was cancelled in 1993, leaving the US Navy with no Hornet, Intruder or Tomcat replacement.

After ATA was cancelled, the US Navy quickly launched the Advanced-Attack/Advanced/Fighter-Attack (A-X/A/F-A) programme, aimed at solving all three issues. The USAF recognised A-X/A/F-A as a possible route to replacing its General Dynamics F-111, McDonnell Douglas F-15E Strike Eagle and Lockheed F-117 Nighthawk fleets, but with the

cancellation of NATF, the US Navy added air-to-air capability to the A-X/A/F-A mission statement, and it became the Advanced Attack/Fighter (A/F-X) programme. The 'lost' A-X, or AX component spawned the Super Hornet, which also took the F-14's fleet defence role, while A/F-X continued as a more distant requirement.

At this point, Congress noticed that both services were involved in multiple programmes with several common requirements. It ordered that they be reconciled. In 1994 therefore, A/F-X and ASTOVL were merged, creating the Joint Advanced Strike Technology (JAST) programme.

In 1996, JAST defined a concept for a new tactical platform and was renamed Joint Strike Fighter (JSF). That same year, the new programme commissioned Boeing to build two X-32 demonstrators and Lockheed Martin two X-35s for a competitive fly-off. Three quite different aircraft models were expected from the winning airframe. As initially imagined, JSF would replace the F-16 with a conventional take-off and landing A-model, the Harrier with a STOVL B-model, and the Intruder and some US Navy and Marine Corps F/A-18C/D Hornets with a carrierborne (CV) C-model. Northrop Grumman and British »

Aerospace joined Lockheed Martin's team in 1997.

Boeing flew first, the X-32A taking the air on September 18, 2000, followed by Lockheed Martin's X-35A on October 24, 2000. Once the 'A' trials had been completed, Lockheed Martin modified the X-35A to X-35B configuration, flying it again on June 23, 2001. Meanwhile, Boeing had flown its dedicated X-32B on March 29, 2001.

Ahead of the CV element, Lockheed Martin had flown its X-35C for the first time on December 16, 2000,

while Boeing used the unmodified X-32A. On October 26, 2001, Lockheed Martin was announced winner of the JSF competition and X-35 became the F-35 Lightning II, 18 years after the ATA programme.

New jet, old problems

Almost 14 more years elapsed before the USMC declared IOC with the F-35B, on July 31, 2015. The UK's first home-based F-35B arrived in-country on June 6, 2018, and the US Navy declared IOC with the F-35C on February 28, 2019. Why

had it taken so long to progress from demonstrator to operational combat aircraft?

The answer to that question is almost as complex as the F-35 itself. At the most basic level, the F-35 programme was expected to produce significantly different variants for operators with quite different requirements while retaining as much similarity between airframes as possible. History had shown the complexities and programme-cancelling pitfalls of such an approach with the F-111 and NATF,

F-35C LIGHTNING II		F-35B LIGHTNING II	
Length	15.70m (51ft 6in)	Length	15.60m (51ft 2.5in)
Wingspan	13.10m (43ft)	Wingspan	10.70m (35ft)
Height	4.48m (14ft 8.5in)	Height	4.36m (14ft 3.5in)
Empty weight	14,651kg (32,300lb)	Empty weight	14,651kg (32,300lb)
Maximum take-off weight, approximately	31,751kg (70,000lb)	Maximum take-off weight, approximately	27,216kg (60,000lb)
Maximum weapon load	8,160kg (18,000lb)	Maximum weapon load	6,800kg (15,000lb)
Maximum speed	Mach 1.6		
Combat radius, internal fuel, more than	1,100km (690 miles)	Combat radius, internal fuel. More than	833km (518 miles)
Engines	One P&W F135-PW-100 turbofan rated at 40,000lb with afterburner	Engines	One P&W F135-PW-600 turbofan rated at 40,500lb with afterburner
Armament	One internal 25mm GAU-22/A cannon, plus weapons bays and pylons for AIM-9X, AIM-120C/D, AGM-154 JSOW, GBU-12 LGB and GBU-31 JDAM. JASSM and LRASM for future integration	Armament	One internal 25mm GAU-22/A cannon, plus weapons bays and pylons for AIM-9X, AIM-120C/D, AGM-154 JSOW, GBU-12 LGB and GBU-31 JDAM. JASSM and LRASM for future integration. UK aircraft compatible with ASRAAM and Paveway IV; SPEAR 3 for future integration
Expected production for carrierborne operations (production continuing)	340	Expected production for carrierborne operations (production continuing)	506

F-35 LIGHTNING II CARRIERBORNE TIMELINE

First flight X-35C – December 16, 2000

First flight X-35B – June 23, 2001

Lockheed Martin declared winner of JSF – October 26, 2001

First flight F-35B – June 11, 2008

First flight F-35C – June 6, 2010

First operational F-35B USMC delivery – November 16, 2012

UK TES established – April 12, 2013

USMC F-35B IOC – July 31, 2015

First UK-based F-35B arrived – June 6, 2018

First USMC combat deployment began – July 2018

First USMC attack – September 27, 2018

US Navy F-35C IOC – February 28, 2019

First UK combat deployment – April 2019

First UK combat mission – June 25, 2019

F-35C introduced to TOPGUN – 2020

First UK cruise – 2021

first USMC F-35C squadron FOC – July 2021

First USN F-35C squadron cruise began – August 2, 2021

First USMC F-35C squadron cruise began – January 9, 2022

Italian Navy FOC expected – December 2024

F-35 LIGHTNING II CARRIERBORNE VARIANTS

X-35B – STOVL demonstrator converted from X-35A, JSF119-PW-611 engine and lift fan, one produced

X-35C – CV demonstrator for JSF competition, JSF119-PW-611 engine, one produced

F-35B – Production STOVL aircraft, F135-PW-100 engine and lift fan, AN/APG-81 AESA radar, production expected 353 for USMC, 138 UK, 15 Italy

F-35C – Production CV aircraft, F135-PW-100 engine, AN/APG-81 AESA radar, production expected 273 for USN, 67 USMC

although the F-4, F/A-18 and, to a lesser extent A-7, had demonstrated that aircraft designed to operate from carriers could successfully fulfil the requirements of air arms ashore.

As the F-35A and, albeit in smaller numbers, F-35B gained export orders, so the already international F-35 programme became a vast multi-national industrial campaign. Adding

to the double challenge of tri-service and international requirements and idiosyncrasy, the F-35 could arguably be considered among the most technologically advanced »

LEFT: Exercise Valiant Shield 2022, in the Philippine Sea on June 15, 2022, and VMFA-121 F-35Bs are busy around the amphibious assault carrier USS *Tripoli*. Compared to the Harrier, advanced flight control systems mean the F-35B is much easier – and safer – to fly close to the ship.
US Marine Corps

RIGHT: Air Test and Evaluation Squadron (VX) 23 engages in a range of USMC and US Navy trials, including this 2023 developmental test work aboard the Royal Navy aircraft carrier HMS *Prince of Wales*. US Navy

aircraft ever brought into service, all of which predictably attracted delays and caused massive cost escalation. Public, political and even military criticism saw the programme threatened with cancellation, but against a backdrop of previously abandoned development programmes and an ageing fleet of Harriers, F-16s and other aircraft, there was little real choice but to carry on.

The US Navy held jurisdiction over the F-35B and F-35C. The F-35B features the Pratt & Whitney F135-PW-600 engine, combined with a forward-mounted Rolls-Royce shaft-driven lift fan. At slow speeds and in the hover, three upper lift fan doors and a pair of underfuselage doors

open to allow air to pass through the fan, while the three-bearing swivel exhaust nozzle is angled downwards, and two roll posts deliver thrust out to the sides for roll control. The lift fan and other equipment related to the F-35B's STOVL capability severely compromises its fuel capacity and, therefore, range compared to the F-35A.

The F-35C uses the same F135-PW-100 engine as the F-35A but is otherwise quite heavily modified for carrier operations. Its wing and control surfaces are larger, their greater area helping reduce the F-35C's landing speed while increasing its range and payload; the wing tips fold for parking aboard ship. The undercarriage

is strengthened and the nose leg equipped with twin wheels, while an arrester hook designed for the rigours of carrier landing replaces the emergency tailhook of the F-35A.

All things considered therefore, it was hardly surprising that the X-35 gained weight as it evolved towards the F-35 variants. The problem was especially acute for the F-35B, but the entire programme was assessed under a weight loss initiative so that the F-35A's first flight was delayed until December 15, 2006; the F-35B flew on June 11, 2008, and the F-35C on June 6, 2010.

Software is key to F-35 capability. The aircraft constantly gathers data from its AN/APG-81 AESA radar, AN/AAQ-37 distributed aperture **»**

ABOVE: Sailors aboard USS *Tripoli* prepare to launch an F-35B in the Pacific Ocean. The aircraft is equipped with rails for AIM-9X under its wing tips.
US Marine Corps

electro-optical and AN/ASQ-239 electronic warfare systems, creating a picture of the battlespace that would overwhelm even the most capable pilot were it not fused for simplified display on the single large cockpit screen and helmet display. Software drives the sensors and displays, and the process of fusion, it is also integral to the flight control system, engine control, navigation and communication functions.

Software has unsurprisingly therefore been responsible for considerably delaying the F-35 programme. Initial operating capability had been expected in 2010, but in 2011 the Department of Defense 're-baselined' the programme for IOC in 2015. The extra time was still insufficient for software development and to avoid further delay, aircraft were delivered to operational squadrons while operational test and evaluation was still under way. Attempting to introduce an aircraft to service while it is still under test is always complicated, doing so while its basic software load is still evolving even more so. The resulting mix of software standards as deliveries continued complicated the in-service fleet and efforts to create a single standard are continuing.

Operational capability

The F-35 is equipped with two weapons bays, each containing a pair of hardpoints. The outboard station is stressed for weapons up to 2,500lb in the F-35C and 1,500lb in the F-35B, while the inner station in each bay accommodates an air-to-air missile. Unlike the F-35A, neither the B- not C-model has an internal gun, although a podded weapon is available where stealth is less important than kinetic effect. In this scenario, underwing pylons add considerably to the weight and scope of weapons at the F-35's disposal.

Among the F-35's still growing customer roster, only the US Navy and Marine Corps are taking the F-35C. The USMC is also the primary F-35B operator, but the variant has found several more customers, among which the UK has already deployed its aircraft at sea, Italy's ITS *Cavour* aircraft carrier is F-35B capable and Japan is modifying its Izumo-class helicopter carriers for the type.

Deliveries of the F-35B and C to the USMC are continuing and the service expects to transition its last squadrons to the type in the 2030/31 timeframe; it used the F-35B in combat for the first time, over Afghanistan, on September 27, 2018. In July 2021, the Corps' VMFA-314 declared full operational capability with the F-35C, beating the US Navy to the milestone but not deploying until 2022. Meanwhile, the US Navy deployed the F-35C

for the first time in August 2021, when VFA-147 embarked in USS *Carl Vinson*.

Such is the potential extent of F-35 capability that its operators are likely to continue learning how best to use it for years to come, especially since it has been designed for continuous upgrade. Its real value comes within a networked combat system, where it acts both as a data gathering and processing vehicle, and information node. Within the context of networked naval operations including the E-2D Advanced Hawkeye and Block III Super Hornet, the US F-35B and C fleets offer unmatched capability.

ABOVE: At rest aboard HMS *Prince of Wales*, a UK F-35B demonstrates the model's humpbacked shape, caused by the lift fan.
LPhot Belinda Alker/ © UK MoD Crown Copyright 2024

LEFT: The larger control surface area of the F-35C is evident as a VFA-147 jet catapults off USS *George Washington* on May 30, 2024.
US Navy

INHERENT RESOLVE AND ODYSSEY LIGHTNING

Carrier aviation first engaged in Operation Inherent Resole in 2014. The commitment continues, a decade later.

Iraq's increasingly perilous security situation as Operation Iraqi Freedom became Operation New Dawn provided an ideal breeding ground for terrorism. The most significant of these organisations, ISIS – later IS, and sometimes Da'esh – seized the Iraqi cities of Mosul and Tikrit in 2014 while engaging in open conflict with Iraqi security forces. US personnel had previously engaged ISIS and their involvement continued under an official title as the terror organisation took control of these geographically separated cities. The US-led Combined

BELOW: A VFA-87 F/A-18E brings a significant weapon load back to USS *George HW Bush* after an OIR mission on June 25, 2017. The ship was stationed in the Mediterranean.
US Navy

Joint Task Force (CJTF) initiated Operation Inherent Resolve (OIR) on June 15, 2014. On September 22, 2014, OIR extended its remit into Syria, where ISIS was also gaining control of territory through the chaos of a civil war raging since Arab Spring protests in 2011.

Combat aircraft operated from land bases in the region and off US Navy aircraft carriers and amphibious assault ships, the French carrier *Charles de Gaulle* and, much later, the new British vessel, HMS *Queen Elizabeth*. Alongside regular US Navy carrier deployments, USS *Kearsarge* launched airstrikes against IS in 2015, and in

June 2016, USS *Harry S Truman* flew attacks from the Mediterranean. Meanwhile, USS *Boxer's* Harriers were working from the Persian Gulf and for the first time US vessels were sending aircraft on OIR missions from both locations simultaneously.

Charles de Gaulle initially joined CJTF-OIR on February 15, 2015, under the French codename Operation Chammal. Stationed in the Persian Gulf, it sent its Rafale Ms and Super Etendards into combat from February 22. The ship left the area in April but deployed again in November. This time it sailed in the Mediterranean, off the Syrian coast. It flew its first

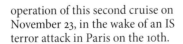

ABOVE: USS *Nimitz* was deployed in the Arabian Gulf in November 2020 when this VAW-116 E-2C was resting between OIR missions. US Navy

LEFT: Aircraft operating off ships in the Mediterranean have the benefit of shorter transits to the Syria area of operations, but combat persistence comes through regular tanking. This Rafale M was refuelling from a USAF KC-135 during an April 2021 OIR sortie. US Air Force

operation of this second cruise on November 23, in the wake of an IS terror attack in Paris on the 10th.

The carrier was back on station in the 'Med' in 2016 as fighting in Iraq intensified, and again in March 2019, when it conducted combat operations early in a longer cruise to Singapore. A COVID outbreak caused its return to port in 2020, but *Charles de Gaulle* was back on OIR duty in 2021.

HMS *Queen Elizabeth* conducted OIR missions during its Carrier Strike Group 21 (CSG21) deployment. The ship embarked UK and US Marine Corps F-35B Lightnings, the former operating over Syria from June 18, 2021, in the UK's first combat missions with the type; the British jets did not release weapons.

Odyssey Dawn

Libya, meanwhile, had failed to find lasting peace after the end of Operation Unified Protector in 2011. IS activity in the country attracted US »

ABOVE: During Operation Odyssey Lightning, USS *Wasp* employed its Harriers, including this aircraft, photographed on September 19, 2016, for precision strikes in support of Libyan Government of National Accord-aligned forces combating IS in Libya. US Navy

RIGHT: Ready to catapult off USS *Nimitz* in the Arabian Gulf during October 2020, this VFA-137 F/A-18E is configured as a tanker, with four drop tanks and a buddy refuelling pod on the centreline. US Navy

attention as early as November 2015, and on August 1, 2016, the US began Operation Odyssey Dawn, a campaign fought similarly to OIR, with the aim of helping Government of National Accord (GNA) forces retake the city of Sirte, which the Libyan arm of IS had claimed as its capital.

Harriers and helicopters operating from USS *Wasp* and USS *San Antonio* provided the GNA with close air support and precision attack. The effort concluded with the effective eradication of IS in Libya on December 19, 2016.

With various regular US troop formations and special forces on the ground establishing and securing forward operating bases, 2017 saw a similar continuation of the air campaign over Iraq and Syria, with a notable exception on June 18, 2017, when VFA-87's Lieutenant Commander Mike 'MOB' Tremel, flying an F/A-18E off USS *George HW Bush*, engaged a Syrian Su-22 *Fitter*.

Working with a joint terminal attack controller (JTAC) on the ground in support of friendly forces in contact with the enemy, Tremel and his wingman attempted to dissuade the Syrian pilot from attacking friendly forces. But the Syrian jet released two bombs, after which Tremel's Sidewinder missed, but the following AIM-120 shot did the job. »

ABOVE: A JDAM-armed Harrier II Plus prepares for an Odyssey Lightning mission off USS *Wasp* on October 12, 2016. US Navy

LEFT: Where there are aircraft carriers and their supporting vessels there are inevitably helicopters. This HSC-6 MH-60S was working with USS *Nimitz* in 2020. US Navy

LEFT: Marines aboard the amphibious transport dock ship USS *San Antonio* for Operation Odyssey Lightning load ordnance on an AH-1W on October 27, 2016. US Navy

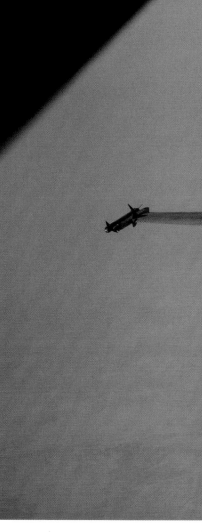

ABOVE: HMS *Queen Elizabeth* embarked F-35Bs from the RAF's 617 Squadron and the USMC's VMFA-211 for CSG21, its inaugural operational cruise. US Navy

RIGHT: This VFA-83 F/A-18C was over Iraq on March 3, 2016, two years before the US Navy retired the type from its carrier decks. US Air Force

RIGHT: A VAQ-130 Growler approaches to refuel from a USAF KC-135 over Iraq on October 5, 2016. The tanker refuelled Belgian F-16 Fighting Falcons during the same mission, such is the international nature of CJTF-OIR. US Air Force

Later in 2017, after three years of hard fighting, IS was considered to have suffered 'territorial defeat' in Iraq. The Iraqi security forces celebrated their victory with a parade on December 9, yet the effort to remove IS personnel and equipment from the country continued in earnest. Through 2018 and into 2019, a concerted effort against IS in Syria resulted in the organisation's 'territorial defeat' being declared on March 23, 2019. Again though, US forces remained in Syria supporting an ongoing campaign against IS.

Since 2019, OIR has seen an increase in insurgent attacks against US bases, using rockets, drones and other weapons. There has also been a CJTF campaign tracking and eliminating IS leaders. Combined Joint Task Force-Operation Inherent Resolve air activity continued at a much reduced intensity in summer 2024; between August 8, 2014, and August 29, 2019, for example, it delivered almost 34,600 attacks. Naval aviation remains essential to this and other air operations in the region.

ABOVE: Three AIM-120, two AIM-9 and two JDAM equip this F/A-18F for any OIR eventuality. It was refuelling form a USAF KC-10A over southwest Asia in August 2017.
US Air Force

UKRAINE AND ISRAEL

Wars in Ukraine and between Israel and Hamas at the eastern end of the Mediterranean, are keeping carrier aviation on alert in the region.

Two very different conflicts have drawn US and French carrier aircraft into the eastern Mediterranean, Adriatic and Aegean Seas in recent years. Russia's annexation of Crimea and subsequent support to separatists fighting government forces in the Donbas region of Ukraine escalated into a full scale invasion on February 24, 2022, when Russian troops crossed into Ukraine from Belarus and Russia.

The conflict has seen bitter fighting as the rapid collapse Moscow may have expected failed to materialise. Ukraine has received massive support in funding, military materiel and training from NATO and other countries and in summer 2024 its resistance remained strong.

Careful not to engage Russian forces directly for fear of catastrophic escalation, NATO moved quickly to reinforce member states surrounding Ukraine and Belarus. The Baltic region and Poland have been a particular focus. Standing fighter patrols were initiated early on, preventing the conflict from 'spilling' beyond Ukraine's borders and protecting the

many NATO intelligence gathering and command and control aircraft operating around Ukraine and Belarus.

Aircraft from the US Navy's Sixth Fleet, part of United States Naval Forces Europe-Africa have been active since the invasion, primarily operating from carriers in the Mediterranean and Aegean. Early in the conflict, Super Hornets, Growlers and Hawkeyes could be monitored on flight tracking websites going about their business alongside other NATO assets, but as the war continued, transponders and other identification aids have often been switched off and these missions have gone 'dark' as far as public tracking is concerned. French carrier aircraft were visible flying patrols from *Charles de Gaulle* during a scheduled Mediterranean cruise known as Clemenceau 22, which sailed on February 1, 2022 and continued into April.

Alongside patrols, and intelligence gathering, NATO assets may have provided targeting information and other data to Ukraine. Some sources suggest that US Navy P-8 patrol aircraft have advised on ship movements,

while the E-2C and EA-18G might also provide useful data.

Israel-Hamas War

On October 7, 2023, Palestinian militant groups led by Hamas crossed from Gaza into Israel to attack civilian and military installations. The action included rocket strikes and killed several people in Israel. The retreating force took with it 251 hostages, reportedly as bargaining chips for the release of Palestinian prisoners.

Israel's response was predictably fast and extreme and the resulting conflict became a prolonged campaign as it raged into summer 2024. The mixed international response included assurances from the US and UK that they supported Israel's right to self-defence. At the same time, the US and other nations have reacted to the humanitarian crisis caused in Gaza by the Israeli offensive, delivering food and other aid.

The US sent USS *Gerald R Ford* into the eastern Mediterranean in response, since when the war has affected the wider region, with attacks against Israel from Hezbollah in Lebanon and Houthi forces in Yemen. Israel ››

BELOW: Flown by another of USS *Harry S Truman's* squadrons, this VAQ-137 EA-18G was over the Aegean Sea on March 1, 2022.
US Navy

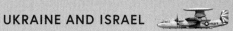

LEFT: Early on in NATO's response to the Ukraine crisis, the US Navy flew fighter patrols over Romania. This VFA-211 F/A-18E flying off USS *Harry S Truman* was refuelling from a German air force A400M over the country on February 25, 2022.
US Navy

LEFT: On March 30, 2022, USS *Harry S Truman* was operating in the Adriatic Sea, where this VFA-211 F/A-18E was about to launch on March 30, 2022.
US Navy

RIGHT: Ejection seat maintenance on a Super Hornet in USS *Harry S Truman*'s hangar bay in June 2022. US Navy

BOTTOM: On March 4, 2022, just 24 days after Russia invaded Ukraine, operations off USS *Harry S Truman* in the Aegean Sea must surely have gained an edge beyond the regular launch and recovery cycle of peacetime carrier operations. US Navy

BELOW: VFA-81 embarked its Super Hornets alongside those of VFA-211 in USS *Harry S Truman* in the immediate aftermath or Russia's invasion of Ukraine. US Navy

has hit targets in Syria, including the Iranian embassy on April 1, 2024, reacting to Iranian support for Houthi militants. The US and other nations have become involved in defending Israel against distant missile and drone strikes, particularly from Yemen and, more recently, Iran. Meanwhile, a Houthi offensive against shipping in the Red Sea and Gulf of Aden off the Yemen coast attracted an international response under Operation Prosperity Guardian.

On April 13, 2024, Iran, working with groups including Hezbollah and the Houthis, mounted a large-scale raid against Israel in retaliation for its attack on the Iranian embassy in

Damascus. Missiles, drones and other weaponry were employed, many of them falling to Israel's Iron Dome air defence system. Several others were shot down by British, French, Jordanian and US fighter aircraft, the latter including US Navy jets. Little damage was caused on the ground.

Neither the war in Ukraine nor the conflict in Gaza seem close to a peaceful conclusion. While the fear of escalation into the wider region continues in both theatres, US aircraft carriers will continue their presence alongside land-based combat assets and the occasional appearance of other nation's carrier-based airpower in the Mediterranean and beyond.

ABOVE: Exercise Neptune Shield 22 demonstrated and practised the ability of NATO maritime forces to conduct integrated operations. Here a VFA-211 F/A-18E refuels an Italian navy F-35B over the Adriatic on May 30, 2022. US Navy

LEFT: This significant show of strength in the Mediterranean on February 25, 2024, includes the Wasp-class amphibious assault ship USS *Bataan*, Harpers Ferry-class dock landing ship USS *Carter Hall*, San Antonio-class amphibious transport dock ship USS *Mesa Verde* and guided-missile destroyer USS *Arleigh Burke* in formation with the Royal Navy primary casualty receiving ship RFA *Argus*. Three Harriers fly ahead of the ships, with AH-1Z helicopters flanking *Bataan*. The vessel has AH-1Z, UH-1Y, MV-22B and Harrier aircraft spotted on its deck, plus a Royal Navy Merlin ready to lift. US Navy

PROSPERITY

The US responded with Operation Prosperity Guardian when the Yemen-based Houthi movement began posing a significant threat to shipping in the Red Sea and Gulf of Aden.

Conflict erupted between Israel and Hamas in Gaza on October 7, 2023, and Yemen's Houthi movement fired missiles and launched drones towards Israel on October 19, before beginning attacks on commercial shipping transiting the Red Sea and Gulf of Aden through the Bab-el-Mandeb strait on November 22.

An attempt to take a ship with Israeli connections on November 26 failed, but anti-ship missiles hit three vessels on December 3. The US claimed the Houthis had Iranian backing and a war of words between the two countries broke out, while the Houthi's declared their intent was to attack shipping connected with Israel until the country allowed humanitarian aid into Gaza.

GUARDIAN

USS *Theodore Roosevelt* was operating in the Red Sea/Persian Gulf/Arabian Sea theatre in summer 2024. This July 31 image shows a VFA-211 F/A-18E about to launch as a tanker.

In fact, the campaign appears to have targeted commercial shipping and military vessels indiscriminately. On December 18, 2023, the US announced its intention to break the blockade through a coalition of forces under Operation Prosperity Guardian. The Coalition faced its first test on December 31, when a container ship came under attack from four smaller vessels. A US

Navy destroyer responded to the attack, along with helicopters from USS *Dwight D Eisenhower*. The aircraft exchanged fire with the attackers, sinking three of them.

On January 10, 2024, the United Nations Security Council added its weight to the crisis, calling for an end to the Houthis action. Coincident with the UN demand, the Houthi's launched their largest attack yet, using drones and

missiles against military ships led by USS *Dwight D Eisenhower* in the Red Sea. The defenders destroyed at least 18 of the incoming threats and there was no damage to vessels.

On January 12, US and UK forces responded with strikes against Houthi targets. US carrier aircraft were involved, alongside British fighters launched from RAF Akrotiri on Cyprus, in Operation Poseidon Archer. »

RIGHT: Armed solely with air-to-air missiles for operations against drones and missiles, a VFA-105 F/A-18E catapults off USS *Dwight D Eisenhower*'s flight deck, in the Red Sea, on April 20, 2024. All US Navy

BELOW: USS *Dwight D Eisenhower* has Super Hornets and Hawkeyes spotted on deck as it transits the Suez Canal towards the Mubarak Peace Bridge on May 5, 2024. The Suez Canal joins the Suez Gulf, at the top of the Red Sea, with the Mediterranean at Port Said, Egypt.

RIGHT: USS *Dwight D Eisenhower* manoeuvres with ships from its carrier group and the Italian aircraft carrier ITS *Cavour* in the Red Sea on June 7, 2024.

BELOW RIGHT: Although Italy reportedly declined to join Operation Prosperity Guardian, ITS *Cavour* exercised alongside USS *Dwight D Eisenhower* in the Red Sea during June 2024. *Cavour* is the smaller and closer of the two vessels.

Houthi efforts appeared undiminished as a missile was fired against USS *Laboon* on January 14 and shot down by a US jet. US Navy Super Hornets appear to have been in action on February 2 when eight drones were downed, but there was no saving *Rubymar* on February 18, after a missile and a submarine drone attack sent the Belize-flagged cargo ship to the bottom. Barbados-flagged *True Confidence* was badly hit on March 6, suffering the first crew fatalities of the crisis; drones sent to attack the crippled vessel under tow two days later were shot down by a French ship and fighters.

On May 31, the Houthis claimed a successful missile attack on USS *Dwight D Eisenhower* after the ship launched aircraft for more strikes on targets in Yemen, but the US Navy responded that no missiles had approached the vessel. A second successful strike, using drones, was claimed for June 1 and another, with missiles, on June 22. On June 12 the Houthis once again caused a sinking, this time of Liberian-flagged *Tutor*, which sank six days later.

Many more attacks have taken place and perhaps hundreds of drones and a variety of missiles have been shot down by warships and aircraft. Operation Prosperity Guardian continued through the summer of 2024 and was undoubtedly providing valuable protection to the international flotilla of ships using these busy waters.

FUTURE UNMANNED?

Militaries the world over are fascinated by uncrewed aircraft, working autonomously or in combination with crewed assets. The US Navy is well on the way to acquiring its first carrier-based UAV, the MQ-25A Stingray.

By the mid-2040s, the US Navy aircraft carrier fleet is likely to comprise a diminishing Nimitz-class fleet in which the youngest carriers are in their final two decades of service, and at least five and perhaps as many as seven or eight Ford-class ships. Their air wings will look familiar to a 2024 naval aviator, however, based on a core of soon-to-be-retired Super Hornet variants and the F-35C, with the latest E-2 Hawkeye variant continuing in its unique role. The major change will be in support, where Boeing's MQ-25A Stingray unmanned air vehicle (UAV) is expected to be flying as a fleet tanker and intelligence-gathering asset. Armed missions are a possibility too.

First flown on September 19, 2019, the MQ-25A has performed tanker 'hook-ups' with the E-2, F-35C and Super Hornet. Unmanned Carrier Launched Multi-Role Squadron 10 (VUQ-10) was established on October 1, 2022, initially for operational test and development but ultimately to become the fleet replacement, or training unit, supplying Stingray crews to the frontline.

Stingray is perhaps the closest of the world's carrier UAVs to service, but other nations are already scheming or testing similar vehicles. Notable among them, China is believed to be flying the GJ-11J unmanned combat air vehicle (UCAV), perhaps as the centrepiece of an air wing equipping a potential UAV-only carrier.

LEFT: A six-hour VX-20 test flight on August 18, 2021 performed fuel transfer and formation evaluations, wake surveys, and drogue tracking and 'plugs' n between MQ-25 T1 and an E-2D, at 220kt and 10,000ft. The combination of MQ-25 with the E-2D, or fast jets, promises tactically significant possibilities for high-risk missions and added combat mass.

LEFT: The first MQ-25, dubbed T1, refuelled an F/A-18F during tr ials on June 4, 2021. All US Navy

BELOW: T1 was trialled aboard USS *George HW Bush* in 2021.